Elevation to Kṛṣṇa Consciousness

ALL GLORY TO SRI GURU AND GAURANGA

ELEVATION TO KRSNA CONSCIOUSNESS

By His Divine Grace
A.C. BHAKTIVEDANTA SWAMI PRABHUPADA
Founder Acharya of the International Society for Krishna Consciousness

THE BHAKTIVEDANTA BOOK TRUST
Los Angeles • London • Paris • Frankfurt • Bombay

Readers interested in the subject matter of this book are invited to correspond with the Secretary (for a full list of temples in each country please see the back of this book):

www.krishna.com

International Society for Krishna Consciousness
P.O. Box 56003, Chatsworth, 4030
S. Africa

International Society for Krishna Consciousness
3764 Watseka Ave, Los Angeles
CA 90034, U.S.A.

International Society for Krishna Consciousness
P.O. Box 262, Botany,
NSW 2019 Australia

ISKCON Reader Services
P.O. Box 730 Watford, WD25 8ZE United Kingdom
Website: www.iskcon.org.uk

Previous Printing: 50,000 copies
Current Printing: 40,000 copies

Printed in Australia by McPherson's Printing Group

ISBN 0-912776-43-9

contents

1

Choosing Human and Animal Lives

oṁ ajñāna timirāndasya jñānāñjana śalākayā
cakṣur unmīlitaṁ yena tasmai śrī-gurave namaḥ

"I offer my respectful obeisances unto my spiritual master, who has opened my eyes, blinded by the darkness of ignorance, with the torchlight of knowledge."

It is customary with this verse to offer obeisances to the spiritual master who enlightens his disciples in the matter of transcendental knowledge. The Vedic process does not involve research work. In mundane scholarship, we have to show our academic learning by some research, but the Vedic process is different. In the Vedic process the research work is already done; it is complete, and it is simply handed down by disciplic succession from teacher to student. There is no question of research work because the instruments and the means with which one conducts such research work are blunt and imperfect.

At this stage of our material existence, we are conditioned by many laws of nature. All conditioned souls are subject to four defects due to the imperfection of their senses. One defect is that the conditioned soul is certain to commit mistakes. There is no man who does not commit mistakes. In India, for instance, Mahātmā Gandhi was supposed to be a very great personality, but he also committed mistakes. Five minutes before he came to the meeting at which he was killed, he was warned by confidential associates not to go, but he persisted. To commit mistakes is very natural in the conditioned state of life. Indeed, the popular saying has arisen: "To err is human."

Another imperfection of the conditioned soul is that he is sure to be illusioned. Being illusioned means accepting something which is not, taking some phantasmagoria to be factual. Every one of us is under the impression that we are these bodies, but actually we are not. Accepting the body to be the self is called illusion, or *māyā*. The third imperfection is that conditioned souls have a tendency to cheat. We have often heard a storekeeper say, "Because you are my friend, I won't make any profit off you." But in actuality we know that he is making at least 50% profit. There are so many instances of this cheating propensity. There are also many examples of teachers who actually know nothing but put forth theories in words like "perhaps" or "it may be," while in actuality they are simply cheating their students. The fourth imperfection is that the senses of the living entity are not perfect. Our vision is so limited that we cannot see very far away nor very near. The eye can see only under certain conditions, and therefore it is understood that our vision is limited. Similarly, all our other senses are also limited. It is not possible to understand the unlimited by these imperfect, limited senses. The conclusion is that the Vedic process does not encourage us to endeavor to learn the Absolute Truth by employing our present senses, which are conditioned in so many ways. If we are to have knowledge, it must come from a superior source which is not conditioned by these four imperfections. That source is Kṛṣṇa. He is the supreme authority of *Bhagavad-gītā,* and He is accepted as the perfect authority by so many saints and sages.

Those who are serious students of Vedic literature accept authority. *Bhagavad-gītā,* for example, is not a scholarly presentation which arose out of so much research work. It is perfect knowledge that was taught by Lord Kṛṣṇa to Arjuna on the battlefield of Kurukṣetra, and we receive information from it that in previous ages Śrī Kṛṣṇa also taught it to the sun-god Vivasvān, and it was handed down from time immemorial from Vivasvān by disciplic succession.

imaṁ vivasvate yogaṁ
proktavān aham avyayam
vivasvān manave prāha
manur ikṣvākave 'bravīt

"The Blessed Lord said: I instructed this imperishable science of *yoga* to the sun-god Vivasvān, and Vivasvān instructed it to Manu, the father of mankind, and Manu in turn instructed it to Ikṣvāku." (Bg. 4.1)

If we study *Bhagavad-gītā* according to academic knowledge or according to our own mental speculation, we are certain to commit mistakes. It is not possible to understand *Bhagavad-gītā* in this way. It is necessary to follow carefully in the footsteps of Arjuna. In previous ages, due to interpretation and mental speculation, the real purport of *Bhagavad-gītā* was lost: therefore Kṛṣṇa re-established the teachings by giving them to Arjuna.

evaṁ paramparā-prāptam
imaṁ rājarṣayo viduḥ
sa kāleneha mahatā
yogo naṣṭaḥ parantapa

sa evāyaṁ mayā te 'dya
yogaḥ proktaḥ purātanaḥ
bhakto 'si me sakhā ceti
rahasyaṁ hy etad uttamam

"This supreme science was thus received through the chain of disciplic succession, and the saintly kings understood it in that way. But in course of time the succession was broken, and therefore the science as it is appears to be lost. That very ancient science of the relationship with the Supreme is today told by Me to you because you are My devotee as well as My friend; therefore, you can understand the transcendental mystery of this science." (Bg. 4.2,3)

Thus whoever follows in the footsteps of Arjuna, approaching Kṛṣṇa in a spirit of devotion, can understand the purpose of *Bhagavad-gītā* as well as all other Vedic literatures.

There are four *Vedas–Sāma, Ṛk, Yajur* and *Atharva,* and there are 108 *Upaniṣads,* including the *Īśopaniṣad, Kaṭha Upaniṣad* and *Taittirīya Upaniṣad,* as well as the *Vedānta-sūtra, Śrīmad-Bhāgavatam* and *Bhagavad-gītā.* These literatures are not meant for any particular class of men but for the totality of human society. All societies can take advantage of Vedic knowledge to perfect human life. As pointed out before, human life is not meant for sense gratification, but for understanding God, the universe and our own identity.

From Vedic literatures we can understand that this material world is only a partial manifestation of the complete creation of God. The larger portion of God's creation is found in the spiritual world of the Vaikuṇṭhas. Above and beyond this material nature there is a superior spiritual nature, as Śrī Kṛṣṇa states in *Bhagavad-gītā:*

bhūmir āpo 'nalo vāyuḥ
khaṁ mano buddhir eva ca
ahaṅkāra itīyaṁ me
bhinnā prakṛtir aṣṭadhā

apareyam itas tv anyāṁ
prakṛtiṁ viddhi me parām
jīva-bhūtāṁ mahā-bāho
yayedaṁ dhāryate jagat

"Earth, water, fire, air, ether, mind, intelligence, and false ego—altogether these eight comprise My separated material energies. Besides this inferior nature, O mighty Arjuna, there is a superior energy of Mine which is all living entities who are struggling with material nature and sustaining the universe." (Bg. 7.4,5)

There are many material universes clustered together, and all these universes constitute the material creation. Beyond these clusters of countless material universes is the spiritual sky, which is also mentioned in *Bhagavad-gītā.*

na tad bhāsayate sūryo
na śaśāṅko na pāvakaḥ
yad gatvā na nivartante
tad dhāma paramaṁ mama

"That abode of Mine is not illumined by the sun or moon, nor by electricity. And anyone who reaches it never comes back to this material world." (Bg. 15.6)

That superior nature which is beyond this material nature is eternal. There is no history of its ever having begun; it has neither beginning nor end.

paras tasmāt tu bhāvo 'nyo
'vyakto 'vyaktāt sanātanaḥ
yaḥ sa sarveṣu bhūteṣu
naśyatsu na vinaśyati

avyakto 'kṣara ity uktas
tam āhuḥ paramāṁ gatim
yaṁ prāpya na nivartante
tad dhāma paramaṁ mama

"There is another, eternal nature, which is transcendental to this manifested and non-manifested matter. It is supreme and is never annihilated. When all in this world is annihilated, that part remains as it is. That supreme status is called unmanifested and infallible, and is the highest destination. Going there, one never returns from that, My supreme abode." (Bg. 8.20,21)

The Vedic religion, or *varṇāśrama-dharma,* is also called eternal because no one can trace out its beginning. The Christian religion has a history of 2,000 years, and the Mohammedan religion has a history of 1,300 years, but if we try to trace out the origins of Vedic religion, we will not be able to find a beginning. *Varṇāśrama-dharma* is accepted as the eternal religion of the living entity.

We often say that God created this material world, and this means that God existed before the world. Since the Lord was existing before this material manifestation, He is not subject to this creation. If He were subject to the laws of the material world, how could He have created it? That the Lord is simultaneously identical with His creation and yet exists in His completeness apart from it is stated in *Bhagavad-gītā.*

mayā tatam idaṁ sarvaṁ
jagad avyakta-mūrtinā
mat-sthāni sarva-bhūtāni
na cāhaṁ teṣv avasthitaḥ

na ca mat-sthāni bhūtāni
paśya me yogam aiśvaram
bhūta-bhṛn na ca bhūta-stho
mamātmā bhūta-bhāvanaḥ

"In My transcendental form I pervade all this creation. All things are resting in Me, but I am not in them. Again, everything that is created does not rest on Me. Behold My mystic opulence: Although I am the maintainer of all living entities, and although I am everywhere, still My Self is the very source of creation." (Bg. 9.4,5)

Actually we are all spirit souls and are intended to associate with God in the spiritual sky where there are innumerable spiritual planets and innumerable spiritual living entities. However, those who are not fit to live in that spiritual world are sent to this material world. This very idea is expressed by Milton in *Paradise Lost.* Although spirit soul, we have voluntarily accepted this material body and by accepting it have also accepted the threefold miseries of material nature. Exactly when we accepted it and how we accepted it cannot be traced out. No one can trace out the history of when the conditioned soul first began accepting these material bodies.

At present Darwin's theory of the evolution of organic matter is very prominent in institutions of higher learning, but there is information given in the *Padma Purāṇa* and other authoritative scriptures of the living entities' spiritual evolution from one bodily form to another. This *Purāṇa* informs us that there are 8,400,000 forms of living entities, 900,000 of which live within water. There are 2,000,000 species amongst plants and vegetables alone. At present everyone is giving stress to Darwin's theory, but in Vedic literature there is immense information about the different species. Darwin expresses the opinion that the species are evolving from lower forms of life, but this is not the whole truth. The soul may progress from lower forms to higher forms, but in the beginning of creation all species were created by Śrī Kṛṣṇa, as indicated in *Bhagavad-gītā.*

sarva-bhūtāni kaunteya
prakṛtiṁ yānti māmikām
kalpa-kṣaye punas tāni
kalpādau visṛjāmy aham

prakṛtiṁ svām avaṣṭabhya
visṛjāmi punaḥ punaḥ
bhūta-grāmam imaṁ kṛtsnam
avaśaṁ prakṛter vaśāt

"O son of Kuntī, at the end of the millennium every material manifestation enters unto My nature, and at the beginning of another millennium, by My potency I again create. The whole cosmic order is under Me. By My will is it manifested again and again, and by My will is it annihilated at the end." (Bg. 9.7,8)

All of these living entities are subject to the threefold miseries, including those miseries pertaining to the body and mind. Animals cannot understand that they are suffering, but human beings can. One who does not know that he is suffering is in animal consciousness. Animals may be standing behind a fence to be slaughtered, but they do not understand this. As human beings, we should be cognizant that we are suffering the pains of birth, old age, disease and death and should be inquisitive to know how to avoid these miseries. We have been suffering from the beginning of our birth when as a baby we were tightly placed for nine months in the womb of a mother. After birth, suffering continues; although a mother may take much care for her child, the baby still cries. Why? Because he is suffering. Either a bug is biting, or there is a pain in the stomach or some other malady. Whatever the case, the suffering goes on. The child also suffers when he is forced to go to school when he does not want to. The child does not want to study, but the teacher gives him tasks anyway. If we carefully analyze our lives, we will find that they are full of suffering. Generally speaking, conditioned souls are not very intelligent, and therefore they go on suffering without ever inquiring why. We should understand, however, that this suffering is there, and if there is a remedy we must take advantage of it.

The great sage Ṛṣabhadeva instructed his sons in this way: "My dear boys, in this life you have acquired these beautiful bodies. Now you should know that they are not meant for sense gratification like the bodies of hogs and dogs but for spiritual realization." Essentially what Ṛṣabhadeva is saying is that a life of sense gratification is meant for stool eaters like hogs, and now that we have a higher form of life, we should not try to imitate the lower forms. Recently we were surprised to see, while walking in Central Park in New York City, that a group of young American boys and girls were engaged in worshiping hogs. While we were chanting Hare Kṛṣṇa, these groups of youngsters were chanting, "Hog! Hog! Hog!" They were actually parading with hogs in Central Park and bowing down before them and worshiping them. They actually wanted one hog to become President, and they wanted the hogs to lead them. This has gone to such lengths that at one be-in in Seattle there was a demonstration with hogs in which the boys and girls undressed themselves and got in the mud and played with the hogs, and in this way they were associating with the hogs and pigs which they worshiped. All this is going on in a country where the young people have good looking bodies, a great deal of money and so many other advantages over the young people of other nations. The result of gaining all these advantages is that they have simply taken to hog worship. Such hog worship was anticipated long, long ago and was described in *Śrīmad-Bhāgavatam,* which was compiled at least 5,000 years ago. The point is that a beautiful situation in life should be utilized for a beautiful end, not for degraded forms of worship.

In the Vedic histories we find that there were many, many exalted emperors and kings who practiced austerities and penances. Dhruva Mahārāja, Ambarīṣa Mahārāja and Yudiṣṭhira Mahārāja were all great kings and were most opulent, but at the same time they were great sages. Thus they set the example for those who have acquired this good opportunity of a beautiful human form of life with all the facilities for economic development and good living. This opportunity should be used to attain an even better life, and this can be actualized by practice of penance. At present we are existing in these material bodies, but if we take to the process of Kṛṣṇa consciousness, our consciousness will be purified. Although American and European, the young students who are voluntarily practicing Kṛṣṇa consciousness are very pleased to practice it. The process is not troublesome but pleasing. Now they are realizing that purified existence constitutes the difference between animal life and human life.

If we purify our existence simply by following the basic regulations of Kṛṣṇa consciousness, which involve abstaining from illicit sexual connection, meat-eating, intoxication and gambling, we will gradually rise to attain our spiritual existence, which is completely pure. The sage Ṛṣabhadeva told his sons that once they purified their existence they would have unlimited happiness. We are all intended to attain peace and happiness, but whatever peace and happiness we find in this material world is limited. If we but purify our existence and attain spiritual existence, we will experience unlimited peace and happiness.

The spiritual world is not dry or abstract; as pointed out before, there is variegatedness there. A part of the spiritual pleasure experienced in the Vaikuṇṭhas is the pleasure of dancing. There are also young girls and young boys there. Indeed, there is no such thing as old age, or disease, or death, or the pains of birth. If we want to participate in the unlimited happiness, knowledge and eternal life which constitute our actual heritage in the spiritual world, we should not waste this life by working hard for sense gratification and worshiping hogs. We should accept a life devoted to the cultivation of Kṛṣṇa consciousness, and then we will get unlimited happiness and unlimited pleasure. This is the sum and substance of the Kṛṣṇa consciousness movement.

2
Hard Struggle for Happiness

In the revealed scriptures the Supreme Lord is described as *sac-cid-ānanda-vigraha. Sat* means eternal, *cit* means fully cognizant, *ānanda* means joyful, and *vigraha* means that He is a person. Thus the Lord, or the Supreme Godhead, who is one without a second, is a fully cognizant and eternally joyful personality with a full sense of His identity. No one is equal to Him or greater than Him. This is a concise description of the Supreme Lord.

The living entities *(jīvas)* are minute samples of the Supreme Lord, and being so they therefore find in their activities the desire for eternal existence, for complete knowledge, and for happiness. These desires are evident in human society, and in the upper planetary systems (Svargaloka, Janaloka, Tapoloka, Maharloka, Brahmaloka, etc.) the living entities enjoy a longer duration of life, an increased amount of knowledge, and a generally more blissful existence. But even in the highest planet in this material world, where the duration of life and standard of enjoyment are thousands and thousands of times greater than those on earth, there is still old age, disease and death. Consequently the level of enjoyment is insignificant in comparison to the eternal bliss enjoyed in the company of the Supreme Lord. Loving service to the Supreme Lord in different relationships makes even the enjoyment of impersonal Brahman as insignificant as a drop of water in comparison to the ocean.

Every living being desires the topmost level of enjoyment in this material world, and yet everyone is unhappy here. This unhappiness is present on all the higher planets, despite a longer lifespan, higher standards of enjoyment and comfort. That is due to the law of material nature. We can increase the duration of life and standard to the highest capacity, and yet by the law of material nature we will be unhappy. The reason for this is that the quality of happiness which is suitable for our constitution is different from the happiness which is derived from material activities. The living entity is a minute particle of the superior spiritual energy of the Lord, which is *sac-cid-ānanda-vigraha,* and therefore he has the necessary propensity for joy which is spiritual in quality. Unfortunately for him, he is trying vainly to attain his enjoyment from the foreign atmosphere of material nature.

A fish that is taken out of the water cannot be happy by any arrangement on land. He must be supplied with water. In the same way, the minute *sac-cid-ānanda* living entity cannot be really happy through any amount of planning conceived by his illusioned brain in this material universe. He must therefore be given a different type of happiness which is spiritual in essence. Our ambition should be aimed at enjoying spiritual bliss and not this temporary happiness. Some philosophers claim that spiritual bliss is attained by negating material happiness and material existence. Theoretical negation of material activities as propounded by Śrīpāda Śaṅkarācārya may be effective for an insignificant section of mankind, but the best and surest way for everyone to attain spiritual bliss was propounded by Lord Śrī Caitanya Mahāprabhu by means of devotional activities. These devotional activities can change the very face of material nature.

Hankering after material happiness is called lust, and lusty activities are sure to meet with frustration in the long run. The body of a snake is very cool, but if a man, wanting to enjoy this coolness, garlands himself with a venomous snake, he will surely be killed by the snake's venomous bite. The material senses are compared to snakes; indulgence in material happiness will surely kill our spiritual identity. Therefore a sane man should be ambitious to find the real source of happiness.

In order to find this source, however, we need some knowledge of what that happiness is. There is the story of the foolish man who had no experience with sugar cane. When he asked his friend about the characteristics of sugar cane, he was imperfectly informed that sugar cane resembles the shape of a bamboo stick. Consequently he began trying to extract juice from bamboo sticks, but naturally he was baffled in his attempts. This is the situation with the illusioned living entity who, in his search for eternal happiness, tries to extract happiness from this material world, which is not only full of miseries but is also transient and flickering. In *Bhagavad-gītā* the material world is described as being full of miseries.

ābrahma-bhuvanāl lokāḥ
punar āvartino 'rjuna
mām upetya tu kaunteya
punar janma na vidyate

"From the highest planet in the material world, down to the lowest, all are places of misery, where repeated birth and death take place. But one who attains to My abode, O son of Kuntī, never takes birth again." (Bg. 8.16)

The ambition for happiness is natural and good, but the attempt to derive it from inert matter by so-called scientific arrangements is an illusory attempt doomed to frustration. Those who are befooled cannot understand this. How a person is driven by the lust for material happiness is also described in *Bhagavad-gītā.*

idam adya mayā labdham
imaṁ prāpsye manoratham
idam astīdam api me
bhaviṣyati punar dhanam

"The demoniac person thinks: 'So much wealth do I have today, and I will gain more according to my schemes. So much is mine now, and it will increase in the future, more and more.' " (Bg. 16.13)

This atheistic or godless civilization is a huge affair contrived for the gratification of our senses, and now we are all mad after money in order to maintain this empty shell. Money is sought after by everyone because that is the medium of exchange for objects for sense gratification. Obviously the expectation of peace in such an atmosphere of gold rush pandemonium is a utopian dream. As long as there is the slightest tinge of sense gratification or desire for sense gratification, peace will remain far, far away. This is because by nature we are all eternal servants of the Supreme Lord and therefore cannot enjoy anything for our personal interests. It is therefore necessary for us to learn how to employ our senses in the transcendental service of the Lord, and to utilize everything to serve His interest. This alone can bring about much desired peace. A part of the body cannot in itself be independently happy. It can only derive its happiness and pleasure out of serving the entire body. The Supreme Lord is the whole, and we are the parts, but we are all busily engaged in activities of self-interest. No one is prepared to serve the Lord. This is the basic cause for our conditioning in material existence and for our resultant unhappiness.

From the highest executive in his skyscraper office down to the coolie in the street—all are working with the thought of accumulating wealth, legally or illegally. Actually it is all illegal, for to work for one's self-interest is both unlawful and destructive. Even the cultivation of spiritual realization for one's own self-interest is unlawful and destructive. The point is that all activities must be directed to the satisfaction of Kṛṣṇa and His service.

Those who are not engaged in the transcendental loving service of the Supreme Lord wrongfully think that they are accumulating so much money day after day.

āśā-pāśa-śatair baddhāḥ
kāma-krodha-parāyaṇāḥ
īhante kāma-bhogārtham
anyāyenārtha-sañcayān

"Being bound by hundreds and thousands of desires, by lust and anger, they secure money by illegal means for sense gratification." (Bg. 16.12)

Consequently, although there is no lack of money in the world, there is a scarcity of peace. So much human energy is being diverted to making money, for the general population has increased its capacity to make more and more dollars, but in the long run the result is that this unrestricted and unlawful monetary inflation has created a bad economy all over the world and has provoked us to manufacture huge and costly weapons to destroy the very result of such cheap money-making. The leaders of the big money-making countries are not really enjoying peace but are making plans to save themselves from imminent destruction by nuclear weapons. In fact, huge sums of money are being thrown into the sea by way of experiments with these dreadful weapons. Such experiments are being carried out not only at huge costs but also at the cost of many lives. In this way the nations are being bound by the laws of *karma*. When men are motivated by the impulse for sense gratification, whatever money is earned is spoiled, being spent for the destruction of the human race. The energy of the human race is thus wasted by the laws of nature because of man's aversion to the Lord, who is actually the proprietor of all energies.

Wealth is worshiped and is referred to as Mother Lakṣmī, or the goddess of fortune. It is her position to serve Lord Nārāyaṇa, the source of all the *naras*, or living beings. The *naras* are also meant to serve Nārāyaṇa under the guidance of the goddess of fortune. The living being cannot enjoy the goddess of fortune without serving Nārāyaṇa, and therefore whoever desires to enjoy her wrongly will be punished by the laws of nature. These laws will make certain that the money itself will bring about destruction instead of peace and prosperity.

Unlawfully accumulated money is now being snatched from miserly citizens by various methods of state taxation for the future civil and international war fund, which is spending money in a wasteful and destructive manner. The citizens are no longer satisfied with just enough money to maintain a family nicely and cultivate spiritual knowledge, both of which are essential in human life. Now everyone wants money unlimitedly to satisfy insatiable desires. In proportion to the people's unlawful desires, their accumulated money is taken away by the agents of illusory energy in the shape of medical practitioners, lawyers, tax collectors, societies, constitutions, so-called holy men, famines, earthquakes, and many similar calamities. One miser who hesitated to purchase a copy of *Back to Godhead* spent $2,000 for a week's supply of medicine and then died. Another man who refused to spend a cent for the service of the Lord wasted thousands of dollars in a legal suit between the members of his home. There are innumerable similar instances occasioned by the dictation of illusory nature. Indeed, that is the law of nature; if money is not devoted to the service of the Lord, it must be spent as spoiled energy in the form of legal problems or diseases. Foolish people do not have the eyes to see such facts; therefore the laws of the Supreme Lord befool them.

The laws of nature do not allow us to accept more money than is required for proper maintenance. There is ample arrangement by the law of nature to provide every living being with his due share of food and shelter, but the insatiable lusts of human beings have disturbed the arrangement set forth by the Almighty Father of all species of life. By the arrangement of the Supreme Lord, there is an ocean of salt because salt is so necessary for the living being. God has, in the same manner, arranged for sufficient air and light, which are also essential. Anyone can collect any amount of salt from the natural storehouse, but constitutionally we cannot take more salt than what we need. If we take more salt, we spoil the broth, and if we take less salt our food becomes tasteless. On the other hand, if we take only what we require, our food is tasty and we are healthy. Presently there is a great deal of concern over the fact that our natural resources are becoming polluted and exhausted. Actually there is ample supply, but due to misuse and greed everything is being spoiled. What conservationists and ecologists do not understand is that everything will continue to be spoiled by the insatiable lusts of mankind unless this Kṛṣṇa consciousness process is taken up. It is impossible to have peace on any platform of existence without Kṛṣṇa consciousness.

Man is therefore suffering due to his insatiable desires and lusts. Not only is man suffering, but the planet on which he resides, his mother earth, represented in *Śrīmad-Bhāgavatam* by mother cow, is also suffering. Once a well-known *svāmī* in India was asked whether God or providence is responsible for the sufferings of humanity. The *svāmī* replied that these sufferings were all God's pastimes or *līlā*. The questioner continued to ask why a living entity should be put under the dictations of the law of *karma*. The *svāmī* could not answer these questions to the satisfaction of his inquirers. The monists and impersonalists who think only in terms of the oneness of the living entities with the Supreme Lord cannot give satisfactory answers to such questions. Such an imperfect reply can hardly satisfy the heart of a living entity.

The Lord is described in all scriptures as *līlā-puruṣottama*, or the Personality of Godhead, who is by His own nature always engaged in transcendental pastimes. In the *Vedānta-sūtra* He is also described as *ānandamayo 'bhyāsāt*. The monists and impersonalists try with great difficulty to explain this *sūtra* in diverse ways in order to support their imperfect theory of oneness and impersonality. However, the fact remains that *ānanda*, pleasure, cannot be enjoyed alone. That variety is the mother of enjoyment is a well-known fact. Cities, for instance, are known to be attractive if they contain a variety of things. Living entities are naturally attracted by variety, by attractive streets, buildings, cinemas, parks, conveyances, businesses, employments, foodstuffs, etc. Despite all this variety, the English poet Cowper once said, "The city is made by man, but the country is made by God." The countryside is also full of natural variegatedness in a crude form, whereas in the city this variegatedness is displayed in a modernized scientific manner. Poets like Cowper are attracted to the variegatedness of the country, and prosaic people who live in the city are attracted by the colorful varieties manufactured by man. In any case, it is variegatedness which attracts people both to the country and the city. This is the proper explanation of the verse of the *Vedānta-sūtra.*

Many so-called *svāmīs* who are so frequently attracted by the cities often seek a kind of pleasure in society and feminine friendship. Generally they are not attracted by the natural beauty of the woods, although they may assume the dress of a man who is meant to live in the woods. Such *svāmīs* are seeking varieties of enjoyment in matter because they have no information of the variegatedness of spiritual life. On the one hand they enjoy variegatedness in matter, and on the other they deny spiritual variegatedness to the Absolute. Because they are pledged to the theory of monism and impersonalism, they deny that whatever pertains to matter can pertain also to spirit. According to them, spirit is the denial of matter. The fact is, however, that spirit is not a negation of matter, but matter is a perverted reflection of spirit.

The real pleasure of variety exists in spirit without deluding relativity. On the other hand, inert matter, in association with dynamic spirit, manifests a false representation or a perverted reflection of that very spiritual variegatedness which is so adamantly denied by the monist class of so-called *svāmīs.*

As stated before, the Supreme Lord is *sac-cid-ānanda-vigraha,* joyful by nature, and therefore He expands Himself by His different energies, parts, and differentiated and plenary portions. The Supreme Lord is the Absolute Truth, and He is one without a second, but He also includes His diverse energies, parts, and plenary portions which are simultaneously one with and different from Him. Because He is joyful by nature, He expands Himself in diverse ways, and the activities of these expansions are called His transcendental pastimes or His *līlā.* These pastimes, however, are not blind and inert; they exhibit full sense, independence, and freedom of action and reaction. The complexities of the actions and the reactions of the diverse energies of the Absolute Truth constitute the subject matter of a vast science called the transcendental science of God, and the *Bhagavad-gītā* is the ABC or primary book of knowledge for students interested in that science. Every intelligent human being should become interested in this transcendental science; indeed, according to the opinions of the sages, human life is only meant for learning this science. The opening words of the *Vedānta-sūtra* proclaim: "Now is the time to inquire about Brahman."

Human life by nature is full of suffering, and lower life forms are even more miserable. Any sane man with properly discriminating senses can understand that life in the material world is full of miseries and that no one is free from the actions and reactions of such miseries. This is not a pessimistic view of life but is an actual fact which we should not be blind to. The miseries of life are divided into three categories, namely miseries arising from the body and mind, miseries arising from other living entities, and miseries arising due to natural calamities. A sane man must look to eliminate these miseries and thereby become happy in life. We are all trying to achieve peace and freedom from these miseries, at least unconsciously, and in the higher intellectual circles there are attempts to get rid of these miseries by ingenious plans and designs. But the power that baffles all the plans and designs of even the most intelligent person is the power of Māyā devī, or the illusory energy. The law of *karma*, or the result of all actions and reactions in the material world, is controlled by this all–powerful illusory energy. The activities of this energy function according to principles and regulations, and they act consciously under the direction of the Supreme Lord. Everything is done by nature in full consciousness; nothing is blind or accidental. This material energy is also called Durgā, which indicates that it is a force which is very difficult to surpass. No one can surpass the laws of Durgā by any amount of childish plans.

To get rid of the sufferings of humanity is simultaneously a very difficult and also a very easy affair. As long as the conditioned souls, who are themselves bound up by the laws of nature, manufacture plans to get rid of the three miseries, there will be no solution. The only effective solutions are those mentioned in *Bhagavad-gītā,* and we have to adopt them in our practical lives for our own benefit. The three miseries of material nature are not found in the pastimes of the Supreme Lord. As mentioned before, He is eternally joyful, and His transcendental pastimes are not different from Him. Because He is the Absolute Truth, His name, fame, form, qualities and pastimes are all identical with Him. His pastimes, therefore, cannot be equated with the sufferings of humanity as the so-called *svāmī* contends. The pastimes of the Supreme Lord are transcendental to the actual miseries and sufferings of human beings.

The sufferings of humanity are caused by the misuse of the discriminative power or the little independence which is given to individual souls. The fraudulent *svāmīs* or mental speculators, in order to remain consistent with the theory of monism, must pass off the miseries of mankind as the pastimes of God, but actually these miseries are only the enforced punishments of Māyā devī inflicted upon the misguided conditioned souls.

As living entities, we are part and parcel of the Supreme Lord. Indeed, we actually belong to His superior energy. As such, we may join His transcendental pastimes in our unconditioned state of life, but as long as we are conditioned by the laws of *karma,* in contact with the inferior energy, our sufferings are our own creations, born of a gross misuse of our little independence. The impersonalist monists only misguide people by contending that the threefold miseries are a part of the Lord's pastimes. Such impersonalists and monists have misguided their followers because they incorrectly think that the Supreme Lord and the individual souls are equal in all respects. True, the individual souls are equal in quality with the Supreme Lord, but not in quantity. If the individual soul were quantitatively equal to the Supreme Lord, he would have never been subjected to the laws of material nature. Material nature is subordinate to the will of the Supreme Lord, and therefore He cannot be subjected to the laws of material nature. It is contradictory for the Lord to be subjected to the laws of His own inferior energy.

mattaḥ parataraṁ nānyat
kiñcid asti dhanañjaya
mayi sarvam idaṁ protaṁ
sūtre maṇi-gaṇā iva

"O conquerer of wealth (Arjuna), there is no truth superior to Me. Everything rests upon Me, as pearls are strung on a thread." (Bg. 7.7)

Again, Śrī Kṛṣṇa states:

tribhir guṇamayair bhāvair
ebhiḥ sarvam idaṁ jagat
mohitaṁ nābhijānāti
mām ebhyaḥ param avyayam

"Deluded by the three modes (goodness, passion, and ignorance), the whole world does not know Me who am above them and inexhaustible." (Bg. 7.13)

The individual souls, who are put into the miseries of the material world, are suffering the resultant reactions of their unsanctioned activities. This is the verdict of *Bhagavad-gītā.*

tān ahaṁ dviṣataḥ krūrān
saṁsāreṣu narādhamān
kṣipāmy ajasram aśubhān
āsurīṣv eva yoniṣu

"Envious, mischievous, the lowest of mankind, these do I ever put back into the ocean of material existence, into various demoniac species of life." (Bg. 16.19)

The parts and parcels are meant to serve the whole, and when they misuse their independence they are subject to the miseries of the laws of matter, just as criminals are subject to police action. The state considers its citizens to be its parts and parcels, and when a citizen misuses his relative independence, the state puts him under police authority. The life of a citizen outside the prison and the life of a citizen within the prison are not the same. Similarly, the sufferings of the living entities within the prison of material nature cannot be equated with the pastimes of the Supreme Lord which exist in the absolute freedom of *sac-cid-ānanda.*

No government wants its citizens to act in such a way that they must go to prison and suffer tribulations. The prisonhouse is undoubtedly constructed by the state government, but this does not mean that the government is anxious for its citizens to be put into it. Indirectly, the disobedient citizens force the government to construct the prisonhouse. It is not done for the pleasure of the government, which has to spend a great deal of money in constructing and maintaining it. On the contrary, the government would be very glad to demolish prisons altogether provided that there are no disobedient citizens in the state. In the same way, this material world is created by the Supreme Lord, but the Supreme Lord does not will that living entities be put in it. The living entities themselves make that decision. The residents of this material world are therefore different from those who are eternally engaged in the transcendental pastimes of the Supreme Lord.

The impersonal monists have no information of full-fledged independent life in the eternal spiritual realm. According to them, the spiritual realm is simply void. This is like prisoners thinking that there is no life outside the prison. Life outside of a prison is certainly free from prison activities, but is not devoid of activity. The soul is by nature eternally active, but the impersonalists try to negate the activities of the soul in the spiritual realm. Thus they misunderstand the miseries of prison life to be the pastimes of the Supreme Lord. This is due to their poor fund of knowledge.

The Supreme Lord never creates the actions and reactions of an individual soul. In *Bhagavad-gītā* this matter is clearly defined in the following way:

na kartṛtvaṁ na karmāṇi
lokasya sṛjati prabhuḥ

na karma-phala-saṁyogaṁ
svabhāvas tu pravartate

nādatte kasyacit pāpaṁ
na caiva sukṛtaṁ vibhuḥ
ajñānenāvṛtaṁ jñānaṁ
tena muhyanti jantavaḥ

"The embodied spirit, master of the city of his body, does not create activities, nor does he induce people to act, nor does he create the fruits of action. All this is enacted by the modes of material nature. Nor does the Supreme Spirit assume anyone's sinful or pious activities. Embodied beings, however, are bewildered because of the ignorance which covers their real knowledge." (Bg. 5.14-15)

It is clear from these passages that the sufferings of humanity are not to be equated with the pastimes of the Supreme Being, nor is the Supreme Being responsible for them. The Lord is never responsible for anyone's vices or virtues. By vicious actions, we are put into more and more distressful conditions, whereas by pious actions we place ourselves on the path of happiness. Thus man is the architect of his own material distress or happiness. The Lord does not want the living entity to become entangled in the reactions of activities, be they good or bad. He simply wants everyone to go back home, back to Godhead. As long as we are not awakened to our pure eternal relation with God, we are certainly bewildered in our actions. Our actions, in respect to right and wrong, are all performed on the platform of ignorance. We must rise to the platform of pure knowledge, which is the pure realization that we are the eternal servitors of the Supreme Lord and enjoyers of His transcendental pastimes. The Supreme Lord is the master-enjoyer of those pastimes, and we are the servitor-enjoyers.

Transcendental knowledge is only attainable by transcendental devotional service, as described in *Bhagavad-gītā.*

teṣāṁ satata-yuktānāṁ
bhajatāṁ prīti-pūrvakam
dadāmi buddhi-yogaṁ taṁ
yena mām upayānti te

"To those who are constantly devoted and worship Me with love, I give the understanding by which they can come to Me." (Bg. 10.10)

By rendering such devotional service only, and not by merely acquiring a bulk of discriminative knowledge, can we know the Supreme Lord as He is. When we know the Personality of Godhead in reality, we can then enter into His pastimes. That is the verdict of all revealed scriptures.

3
Toward a Peaceful Society

śrī bhagavān uvāca
idaṁ śarīraṁ kaunteya
kṣetram ity abhidhīyate
etad yo vetti taṁ prāhuḥ
kṣetrajña iti tad-vidaḥ

"The Supreme Lord said: This body, O son of Kuntī, is called the field, and one who knows this body is called the knower of the field." (Bg. 13.2)

The Supreme Personality of Godhead, Kṛṣṇa, is instructing Arjuna about the knowledge of *kṣetra* and *kṣetrajña. Kṣetra* refers to the field, which is the body, and *kṣetrajña* refers to the knower of the field, who is the individual soul. If land is to be cultivated, there must be some cultivator, and if this body, which is likened unto a field, is to be cultivated, there must be a proprietor who can cultivate it. Now we have these material bodies, and it is our duty to cultivate them properly. That cultivation is called *akarma,* or work. A person may come to our place with a hoe to cultivate land, or he may come to simply drink coffee or tea. We have been given this particular type of body to cultivate and to attain required sense objects according to our desires. This body is a gift from God. God is very kind, and if someone wants something from Him, He allows it. "All right," He says. "Take this." His relationship to us is just like the relationship of a father to a son. The son may insist upon getting something from the father, and the father may try to convince him that what he wants is not for his good, saying, "My dear son, don't touch this. This is not good for you." But when the boy insists upon it, the father will allow him to have it. The affectionate father gives the son just what he wants. Similarly, the Supreme Father gives His sons and daughters just what they want. It is stated in *Bhagavad-gītā* that all beings, in all species of life, are his children.

sarva-yoniṣu kaunteya
mūrtayaḥ sambhavanti yāḥ
tāsāṁ brahma mahad yonir
ahaṁ bīja-pradaḥ pitā

"It should be understood that all species of life, O son of Kuntī, are made possible by birth in this material nature, and that I am the seed-giving Father." (Bg.14.4)

In this material world, the mother, *prakṛti,* which is material nature, supplies us with the body, and the Supreme Father impregnates this matter with living souls. There is an erroneous theory current that only human beings have souls and that other living entities do not, but we understand from Vedic authority that there are over 8,000,000 species of bodies, including plants and trees, and that they all have souls, otherwise they would not be able to develop and grow. In this verse Śrī Kṛṣṇa claims that all living entities, regardless of the forms they take in this material world, are his sons, and that they are related to Him as a son is related to his father.

This Kṛṣṇa consciousness is especially meant for understanding the position of the soul and its relationship with God.

kṣetrajñaṁ cāpi māṁ viddhi
sarva-kṣetreṣu bhārata
kṣetra-kṣetrajñayor jñānaṁ
yat taj jñānaṁ mataṁ mama

"O scion of Bharata, you should understand that I am also the knower in all bodies, and to understand this body and its owner is called knowledge. That is My opinion." (Bg. 13.3)

If we meditate upon this body and study whether or not we are actually the body, we will come to the conclusion that we are *kṣetrajña,* the knower of the body but not the body. If we study our finger and consider whether or not we are the finger, we will come to the conclusion that we are not the finger or any other part of the body, but that the finger, the arms, the legs, the head, etc. are *our* fingers, arms, legs, etc. In this way we can come to the conclusion that we are not these bodies but that the bodies belong to us. Therefore we say, "This is my body." Unfortunately people in this modern civilization never stop to inquire what they are or who they are. They are simply laboring hard, working hard all day in an office or factory, under the impression that, "I am this body." And if we ask people who they are, they reply, "I am Hindu, I am Moslem, I am Swedish, I am American, I am Christian, etc." These are various identifications or designations of the body, but the fact is that we are not these bodies. The body is simply the field of our activities. We are no more the body than the cultivator of a field is the field.

There are different kinds of bodies and different activities in accordance to the different types of bodies. A dog enjoys one kind of activity, a cat enjoys another, and a human enjoys another. There are differences of activity due to differences of body. When we come to the platform of truth, however, and understand that we are not these bodies, then our activities change from material activities to spiritual activities. As long as we are operating under the bodily conception of life, our activities are material, but as soon as we understand, "I do not belong to this body, *ahaṁ brahmāsmi,* I am spirit soul," our activities will be in accordance to that realization, that is to say that they will cease to be motivated from the material or bodily platform. Knowledge of our proper identity as separate from the body is real knowledge, but this knowledge is denied as long as we cling to bodily identification.

In the scriptures it is said that as long as we are in this bodily conception of life, all our activities will be defeated. A child is born into ignorance, and if as he grows older he remains under the bodily conception of life, he lives in darkness. His position is that of a *śūdra.* In the Vedic literatures we find that in this age everyone is born a *śūdra;* therefore everyone requires to be educated as to his real identity. If, however, we remain satisfied with our birth by our father and mother, we will remain in our condition as *śūdra.* We have to rise to the brahminical platform by following the purificatory processes.

As mentioned before, there are four basic characteristics of an impure life—illicit sex, intoxication, meat-eating and gambling. According to the Vedic principles, sex should not be indulged in outside of marriage. In human society there is therefore a system of marriage which distinguishes us from the cats and dogs. Whether we are Hindu, Moslem, or Christian, we acknowledge the system of marriage. The purpose of this system is to avoid illicit sex. According to the Vedic system, intoxication is also discouraged; nor is meat-eating advocated, for human beings should be nonviolent. We have been given sufficient grains, fruits, milk, and vegetables, and there is no necessity to kill poor animals. Some people argue that if we do not eat meat we will be undernourished, but we can see that the students of this Kṛṣṇa consciousness movement have given up meat and are very healthy, whereas people who are eating meat are still, despite their meat-eating, subject to so many diseases and unhealthy conditions. Gambling is also discouraged because it simply agitates the mind.

This then is the purificatory process by which one can become a *brāhmaṇa.* This path is open to everyone. A *brāhmaṇa* is one who is truthful and pure, tolerant and simple, full of knowledge and faith in God. He can control his mind and his senses also. At the present moment there is a great necessity for *brāhmaṇas,* because almost everyone is a *śūdra,* for almost everyone is wholly engaged in maintaining the body, eating, sleeping, mating and defending–all symptoms of animals and *śūdras.*

Society cannot be peaceful unless there are four divisions of human beings functioning in harmony with one another. These four divisions are comprised of *brāhmaṇas, kṣatriyas, vaiśyas* and *śūdras.* These are discussed by Kṛṣṇa in *Bhagavad-gītā* in this way:

cātur-varṇyaṁ mayā sṛṣṭaṁ
guṇa-karma-vibhāgaśaḥ
tasya kartāram api māṁ
viddhy akartāram avyayam

"According to the three modes of material nature and the work ascribed to them, the four divisions of human society were created by Me. And, although I am the creator of this system, you should know that I am yet the non-doer, being unchangeable." (Bg. 4.13)

These four divisions of men in human society are natural, not artificial, because in the material world everything is operating under the influence of the three modes of material nature–goodness, passion and ignorance. As long as we are in the material world, it is not possible to classify everyone in the same category because each and every person is working under the influence of the modes of material nature. However, when we transcend the material plane, there is oneness. At that time, all the divisions fall apart. The question is therefore how to transcend the modes of material nature, and that transcendence is the very process of Kṛṣṇa consciousness. As soon as we become situated in Kṛṣṇa consciousness, we become transcendental to the modes of material nature.

māṁ ca yo 'vyabhicāreṇa
bhakti-yogena sevate
sa guṇān samatītyaitān
brahma-bhūyāya kalpate

"One who engages in full devotional service, who does not fall down in any circumstance, at once transcends the modes of material nature, and thus comes to the level of Brahman." (Bg. 14.26)

Thus one who is engaged in Kṛṣṇa conscious activity is at once elevated to the transcendental position. By nature we are not matter but Brahman *(ahaṁ brahmāsmi)*. The philosophy of Śaṅkarācārya is mainly based on the principle that we should not think that we are products of this material nature. It is by some unfortunate accident that we are in contact with material nature. Actually our nature is that of spirit, Brahman, and that nature has to be invoked. This material life is a diseased condition; when we are situated in Brahman, we are in our healthy condition. That healthy Brahman condition is immediately attained as soon as we engage ourselves one hundred percent in Kṛṣṇa consciousness.

When we transcend material nature through the rendering of service unto Kṛṣṇa, what is our status? Do we become zero? Some philosophies maintain that after liberation from material life, after the *nirvāṇa* of this material body, we become zero, void. That is a dangerous theory. By nature the living entity is not attracted to zero. We may be diseased and suffering from so many elements, but if our doctor comes and says, "Let me finish your ailments by killing you," we will immediately say, "No, no! Better let me suffer from the disease." We do not want to be killed just to end our miseries. Thus the theory that after material life there is void is not at all attractive. Nor is it a fact. We are *sac-cid-ānanda-vigraha,* eternal, blissful and full of knowledge, and part and parcel of the Supreme. The Supreme Lord is *sac-cid-ānanda-vigraha,* and we are qualitatively one with Him. Although very small, a drop of seawater is as salty as the sea, and although we are but spiritual atoms, we have the same properties as the supreme spirit whole. There is no question of being void, for as living entities our spiritual properties are all there in infinite variegatedness. If, however, out of the frustration of material existence we commit suicide, we do not end our miseries. We simply create other miseries. If one attempts suicide but does not succeed, or is somehow revived, he is subject to being punished under state law. Similarly, the laws of nature treat suicides as criminal acts. We are to end this material life only after finding out the true blissful life of eternity. We should not simply be trying to end the miseries of this life simply out of frustration, but we should engage ourselves in activities that will raise us to spiritual life.

The four divisions of human society were created by Śrī Kṛṣṇa in order to facilitate this process of elevation. Just as a student is elevated from a lower class to a post-graduate class, the divisions of labor *(cātur-varṇyam)* are created to elevate us from the lowest stages of consciousness to the highest stage of Kṛṣṇa consciousness. This process is a process of cooperation. In the human body, the most important part is the head, then the arms, the belly and the legs. Although the head is considered to be the most important part, there is no question of neglecting the legs or any other part. Similarly, in the divisions of human society, no one division is important to the exclusion of the others. Of these divisions, the *brāhmaṇas* are considered to be the intellectual class, the class of teachers; the *kṣatriyas* are the administrative and military class; the *vaiśyas* are the mercantile and agricultural class; and the *śūdras* are the common laborer class. In a properly run society, all of these classes are required. If they cooperate in their progress toward Kṛṣṇa consciousness, there is no strife amongst them.

In the present social status, we find that we are existing in these four divisions, but there is no cooperation. Everyone is dissatisfied. Today there is great strife between the capitalist class and laborer class because between them there is no compromise. There is only friction. All this strife amongst the classes is due to lack of Kṛṣṇa consciousness. Indeed, there is not even a possibility of cooperation unless there is Kṛṣṇa consciousness. Kṛṣṇa consciousness is absolutely essential for harmonizing all facets of human society. Regardless of what class we belong to, if we cooperate in Kṛṣṇa consciousness, there will be peace in the world.

Thus Kṛṣṇa consciousness is the utmost necessity for all divisions of society. Every chapter and every conclusion of *Bhagavad-gītā* aim toward Kṛṣṇa consciousness. Śrī Kṛṣṇa, who is speaking *Bhagavad-gītā*, is always stressing devotion to His personal Self.

manmanā bhava madbhakto
mad-yājī māṁ namaskuru
mām evaiṣyasi satyaṁ te
pratijāne priyo 'si me

"Always think of Me and become My devotee. Worship Me and offer your homage unto Me. Thus you will come to Me without fail. I promise you this because you are My very dear friend." (Bg. 18.65)

Throughout *Bhagavad-gītā* we find this word *mām* stressed. *Mām* means "unto Me," meaning unto Kṛṣṇa. But there are many miscreants who are interpreting this *mām* to mean "everyone." When I say, "Bring me a glass of water," does it mean that I want you to bring everyone a glass of water? The individuality is there, but by jugglery of words they interpret "me" or "I" to mean "everyone." Consequently when Kṛṣṇa says "I," the miscreants identify this "I" with themselves. This is a gross misinterpretation. Although *Bhagavad-gītā* is very popular in the world, due to this misinterpretation by mundane scholars, it has not been properly understood.

Bhagavad-gītā clearly explains that this *cāturvarṇyam* system was established by Kṛṣṇa, but He is outside of this system. When Kṛṣṇa comes as an incarnation, He does not come as a member of any social order, not as a *brāhmaṇa* or anything else. When Kṛṣṇa came, He came as the son of Devakī and Vasudeva. Vasudeva belonged to the royal family and was therefore a *kṣatriya.* As such, Kṛṣṇa played the part of a *kṣatriya,* but this does not mean that Kṛṣṇa belonged to the *kṣatriya* class. There are many incarnations of Kṛṣṇa in many forms of life. In one incarnation He appeared as a fish, as a member of the community of fishes, but this does not mean that He is a fish. If we think upon seeing a fish that it belongs to Kṛṣṇa's family, we arc mistaken. Of course, from another point of view, everything is Kṛṣṇa, but Kṛṣṇa is aloof from everything. This is the transcendental nature of Kṛṣṇa, and if we understand it, we will be liberated from birth and death. Although Kṛṣṇa has established the four divisions of human society, He is not in any one of them *(tasya kartāram api māṁ viddhy akartāram avyayam).* As soon as we understand that although Kṛṣṇa was born into a *kṣatriya* family, He is not a *kṣatriya,* we actually become liberated. If we think that because Kṛṣṇa acts in a particular way—as on the battlefield He gave instructions to Arjuna to fight—He is bound by the reactions of His activities, we are mistaken. "Works do not defile Me," Śrī Kṛṣṇa says *(na māṁ karmāṇi limpanti).* In conclusion, we must accept the fact that when Kṛṣṇa comes as one of us, He is not in actuality "one of us." He is transcendental. This fact we must learn by submissive inquiry from authoritative sources, such as *Bhagavad-gītā* or a spiritual master who is fully realized in Kṛṣṇa consciousness.

Today all facets of human society are thinking that their self-interest is in maintaining this body. Consequently today's society is simply a society of cats, dogs and hogs. From Vedic literatures we can understand that we don't have to work hard all day simply to maintain this body. We are working very hard because we are trying to control material nature for the purposes of sense gratification. One who can come to understand that Kṛṣṇa is the root of everything, the origin of everything, can understand the meaning of *īśvaraḥ paramaḥ kṛṣṇaḥ*—Kṛṣṇa is the supreme controller. In the universe there are many *īśvaras,* or controllers, but Kṛṣṇa is the supreme among all of them. Kṛṣṇa consciousness gives us this knowledge. Without it, we will remain ignorant of our real self-interest.

Modern society is in dire need of intellectual persons or *brāhmaṇas* who can broadcast real spiritual knowledge all over the world. That is an absolute necessity for a society which is working hard simply to exploit nature. If people try to understand this Kṛṣṇa consciousness movement scientifically and philosophically, with their best knowledge and judgement, and try to cooperate, there will be peace all over the world. In essence, the method is very simple. We need only chant Hare Kṛṣṇa, Hare Kṛṣṇa, Kṛṣṇa Kṛṣṇa, Hare Hare / Hare Rāma, Hare Rāma, Rāma Rāma, Hare Hare and follow the regulative principles mentioned before. By following the regulative principles, we will be avoiding the four pillars of sinful life, and by chanting the Hare Kṛṣṇa *mantra,* we will be associating with God constantly; thus there will be peace among all classes of men.

4
Knowing Kṛṣṇa as He Is

We do not need any high qualifications to offer prayers to the Supreme Personality of Godhead. Whatever our social or intellectual position may be, we can offer prayers. We do not have to be very learned or very scholarly, nor do we have to present our prayers in nicely selected words that are poetical, rhetorical or metaphorical. None of this is required, although if it is there it is very nice. We simply have to express our feelings, but in order to be able to do this we have to be aware of our position. Once we are aware of our position, our feelings can be expressed sincerely and automatically.

What is our position? This has been taught by Lord Caitanya Mahāprabhu, who teaches us how to pray in his prayer:

na dhanaṁ na janaṁ na sundarīṁ
kavitāṁ vā jagadīśa kāmaye
mama janmani janmanīśvare
bhavatād bhaktir ahaitukī tvayi

"O almighty Lord! I have no desire to accumulate wealth, nor have I any desire to enjoy beautiful women, nor do I want any number of followers. What I want only is that I may have Your causeless devotional service in my life–birth after birth." *(Śikṣāṣṭakam, 4)*

In this prayer the word *jagadīśa* means "Lord of the universe." *Jagat* means universe, and *īśa* means

Lord. Whether we are Hindu, Moslem or Christian or whatever, we must acknowledge that there is a supreme controller of this universe. This cannot be denied by anyone who has faith in God. Our conviction should be that our Supreme Father is Jagadīśa, or Lord of the entire universe. Only Lord Jagadīśa is in control; everyone else is controlled. The atheists, however, do not like this term because they like to think that they are in control, but actually this is not the case. All beings in the material world are subject to the three modes of material nature—goodness, passion and ignorance—but the Supreme Lord is above these modes.

tribhir guṇamayair bhāvair
ebhiḥ sarvam idaṁ jagat
mohitaṁ nābhijānāti
mām ebhyaḥ param avyayam

"Deluded by the three modes (goodness, passion, and ignorance), the whole world does not know Me who am above them and inexhaustible." (Bg. 7.13)

The *Brahma-saṁhitā* also gives us information regarding Jagadīśa, the Supreme. In that work, Lord Brahmā says that the supreme controller is Lord Kṛṣṇa Himself *(īśvaraḥ paramaḥ kṛṣṇaḥ)*. The word *īśvaraḥ* means controller, and the word *paramaḥ* means supreme. All of us are controllers to some limited extent. If we have nothing to control, sometimes we keep a dog or cat so we can say, "My dear dog, please come here." In this way we can think, "I am the controller." Sometimes the tables turn, however, and we find that the dog controls the master. This happens because actually no one is the controller, and everyone is controlled. Unfortunately we are forgetful of this situation, and this forgetfulness is called *māyā.* We refuse to accept any controller of this universe because if we accept a controller we have to account for our sinful activities, just as when we accept the government we have to account for our unlawful activities. Our position is that we want to continue in our sinful activities, and therefore we deny the existence of a controller. This is the basic principle of godlessness. The current propaganda that "God is dead" is spread because people want to continue being rascals without restriction. This is the basic principle underlying the denial of God's existence. But however much we deny His existence, He will not die. In this regard, there is a Bengali proverb that says: *śakuni śāpe gorumaraṇa.* The work *śakuni* means vulture. Vultures enjoy dead animal carcasses, especially the carcass of the cow. Sometimes a vulture may go for days without a carcass; therefore this proverb says that the vulture curses the cow, wishing him to die. But this does not mean that the cow will die just to oblige the vulture. Similarly, these atheistic vultures want to see God dead so they can take pleasure in thinking, "Now God is dead, and I can do anything I like."

We must know then for certain that there is a controller; that is the beginning of knowledge. Why should we deny this truth? In every field of activity we find some finite controller, so how can we deny the existence of an infinite controller in this creation? It is not without reason therefore that Lord Caitanya

Mahāprabhu particularly uses this word Jagadīśa, Lord of the universe. He does not manufacture the term, for it is found in many different Vedic *mantras.* For instance:

tava kara-kamala-vare nakham adbhuta-śṛṅgaṁ
dalita-hiraṇyakaśipu-tanu-bhṛṅgam
keśava dhṛta-narahari-rūpa jaya jagadīśa hare

"O my Lord, Your hands are very beautiful, like the lotus flower, but with Your long nails You have ripped apart the wasp Hiraṇyakaśipu. Unto You, Lord of the universe, do I offer my humble obeisances."

Hiraṇyakaśipu was an atheist who denied the existence of God, but God came as Lord Nṛsiṁhadeva, a half-man, half-lion incarnation, and killed him. Therefore praise is given to the Lord as supreme controller of the universe and all living entities *(jaya jagadīśa hare).*

There is also another prayer: *jagannātha-svāmī nayana-patha-gāmī bhavatu me:* "O Lord of the universe, please be visible unto me." In all these prayers, and in many others, the supreme controller of the universe is acknowledged. Everyone is trying to become supreme controllers, but it is not possible by individual, communal or national effort. Because everyone is trying to be supreme, there is great competition in the world. The world is created in such a way, however, that no one can become supreme. Regardless of what position we place ourselves in, we will find that someone is inferior to us and that someone is superior. No one individual can say, "I am the supreme. No one is above me." Nor can anyone say, "I am the most inferior. No one is below me." Once we think that we are the most inferior, we'll immediately find that someone is inferior to us; and once we think that we are supreme, we'll immediately find someone superior. This is our position.

God's position, however, is not like this. In *Bhagavad-gītā* Kṛṣṇa asserts His superiority Himself in this way:

mattaḥ parataraṁ nānyat
kiñcid asti dhanañjaya
mayi sarvam idaṁ protaṁ
sūtre maṇi-gaṇā iva

"O conquerer of wealth (Arjuna), there is no truth superior to Me. Everything rests upon Me, as pearls are strung on a thread." (Bg. 7.7)

God is *asamaurdha,* which means that no one is equal to or superior to Him. If we find someone who has no superior, we can accept him as God. God can be defined as one who has no superior and who has no equal. This is the Vedic version. In the Upaniṣads it is said, *na tat samaś cābhyadhikaś ca dṛśyate:* no one is found equal to or greater than Him.

Another characteristic of God is that He has nothing to do. In the material world, when a man is considered very important, he always has a great number of things to do. The President of the United States, for instance, is considered to be the supreme man in the country, but as soon as there is some disturbance in Central Europe or in any other place in the world, he immediately has to call a meeting of his cabinet to consider how to deal with the situation. So even he is required to do so many things. If he does not do anything, he is no longer the supreme man. In Vedic literatures, however, we find that God has nothing to do *(na tasya kāryaṁ karaṇaṁ ca vidyate).* Kṛṣṇa may act in so many ways in the world, but it is not because He is required to do so. This is indicated in *Bhagavad-gītā.*

na me pārthāsti kartavyaṁ
triṣu lokeṣu kiñcana
nānavāptam avāptavyaṁ
varta eva ca karmaṇi

"O son of Pṛthā, there is no work prescribed for Me within all the three planetary systems. Neither am I in want of anything, nor have I the need to obtain anything—and yet I am engaged in work." (Bg. 3.22)

In this respect it is interesting to note that one European gentleman, who went to Calcutta and visited several temples, noted that in the temple of the goddess Kālī, the deity had a very ferocious figure, with a chopper in hand, and was cutting off the heads of demons and wearing them as garlands. In other temples he saw the deity engaged in similar activities, but when he came to the Rādhā-Kṛṣṇa temple, he said, "I find that in this temple there is God." When asked how he concluded this, he said, "In every temple I saw that the deity was doing something, but here I see that God is simply playing a flute and enjoying Himself. He obviously has nothing to do." This is a very intelligent conclusion; indeed, it is the Vedic conclusion.

Nowadays it is becoming fashionable for people to claim that they are becoming God by meditation. This means that by meditation it is possible to transform oneself into God; in other words, God meditates, and by His meditation He becomes God. This is all nonsense. God is God, and He was always God and will always be God. Even as an infant on the lap of His mother Kṛṣṇa is God. No meditation was required, no austerity or penance. When Pūtanā, the demonic witch, came to poison Baby Kṛṣṇa, she came as a beautiful young girl and asked Mother Yaśodā, "Oh, Yaśodāmayī, you have a very nice baby. Will you kindly give Him to me so I can nurse Him?" Yaśodā was a very simple village woman, and she said, "Oh yes, you can take my child." Pūtanā had smeared poison on her breasts, and she intended to kill Kṛṣṇa by letting Him suck them. This is the demonic spirit; demons are always wanting to kill Kṛṣṇa so they can say, "God is dead. There is no God. God is impersonal." Kṛṣṇa was so kind to Pūtanā that He allowed her to nurse Him, but when He sucked her breasts He not only sucked out the poison but her life as well. Pūtanā fell to the ground dead and was immediately transformed into her original demonic form. So this is God; in the lap of His mother He is God. He does not have to become God by meditation, penance, austerity or by following rules or regulations. He is substantially and eternally God, and He has nothing to do. If one claims that he can become God by worshiping such and such a deity or by meditating, we should immediately take it that he is not a god, but a dog. In understanding God, we must be careful to accept the Vedic conclusion only: *na tasya kāryaṁ karaṇaṁ ca vidyate:* God has nothing to do. Why would God have to do something to become God? If we manufacture gold, that is artificial gold, not real gold. Gold is natural, and similarly God is natural. In His childhood pastimes, in the lap of His mother, He is God; while He is playing with His boyfriends, He is God; while He is dancing, He is God; while He is fighting at Kurukṣetra, He is God; while He is married to His queens, He is God; and while He is speaking, He is God. There is no difficulty in understanding God. All that is required of us is that we listen to Kṛṣṇa.

In *Bhagavad-gītā* Kṛṣṇa tells Arjuna:

ahaṁ sarvasya prabhavo
mattaḥ sarvaṁ pravartate
iti matvā bhajante māṁ
budhā bhāva-samanvitāḥ

"I am the source of everything; from Me the entire creation flows. Knowing this, the wise worship Me with all their hearts." (Bg. 10.8)

This means that Śrī Kṛṣṇa is the fountainhead of Lord Śiva and the origin of Viṣṇu and of Brahmā, and, of course, of all other demigods and other living creatures. He says further:

mamaivāṁśo jīva-loke
jīva-bhūtaḥ sanātanaḥ
manaḥ-ṣaṣṭhānīndriyāṇi
prakṛti-sthāni karṣati

"The living entities in this conditional world are My fragmental parts, and they are eternal. But due to conditioned life, they are struggling very hard with the six senses, which include the mind." (Bg. 15.7)

In the *Brahma-saṁhitā* Lord Brahmā explains that if we are looking for God, here is God.

premāñjana-cchurita-bhakti-vilocanena
santaḥ sadaiva hṛdayeṣu vilokayanti
yaṁ śyāmasundaram acintya-guṇa-svarūpaṁ
govindam ādi-puruṣaṁ tam ahaṁ bhajāmi

"I worship Govinda, the primeval Lord, Who is Śyāmasundara, Kṛṣṇa Himself, with inconceivable innumerable attributes, whom the pure devotees see in their heart of hearts with the eye of devotion tinged with the salve of love." (*Bs.* 5.38)

There are similar descriptions everywhere in Vedic literature, but rascals and demons are so obstinate that even though Kṛṣṇa is confirmed to be the Supreme God by the twelve standard *ācāryas* (Brahmā, Nārada, Śiva, Bhīṣma, the Kumāras, Kapila, Manu, etc.) and by Vyāsa, Devala and many other devotees, they still refuse to accept Him. Lord Caitanya Mahāprabhu also confirms that Kṛṣṇa is the Supreme Godhead, and the *Śrīmad-Bhāgavatam* says, *kṛṣṇas tu bhagavān svayam. Śrīmad-Bhāgavatam* gives a list of all incarnations of God, and at last concludes that the name Kṛṣṇa, which appears on this list, indicates the Supreme Personality of Godhead, whereas all other names represent manifestations or incarnations. *Ete cāṁśa-kalāḥ puṁsaḥ.* All other names of God are either parts of God or portions of parts. The parts are called *aṁśa,* and the portions of parts are called *kalāḥ.* As living entities, we are *aṁśa,* but we are very fragmental *aṁśa.* All others are either *aṁśa* or *kalāḥ,* but Kṛṣṇa is *bhagavān svayam*—the Supreme Personality of Godhead.

Our prayers should be directed to the Supreme Personality of Godhead and none else. Therefore we pray with Brahmā:

cintāmaṇi-prakara-sadmasu kalpa-vṛkṣa
lakṣāvṛteṣu surabhīr abhipālayantam
lakṣmī-sahasra-śata-sambhrama-sevyamānaṁ
govindam ādi-puruṣaṁ tam ahaṁ bhajāmi

"I worship Govinda, the primeval Lord, the first progenitor, who is tending the cows, fulfilling all desire, in abodes built with spiritual gems, surrounded by millions of wish-fulfilling trees, always served with great reverence and affection by hundreds of thousands of Lakṣmīs, or *gopīs.*" (*Bs.* 5.29)

Here Kṛṣṇa is called the original person *(ādi-puruṣam).* We are all persons. Our father is a person, and therefore we are persons. If we trace our father's father back, we will find that he was also a person, and that his father was a person, and so on all the way back to Lord Brahmā, who was the first created person in this universe. Then we will also find that Lord Brahmā's father, Viṣṇu, is also a person. Everyone is a person, and Kṛṣṇa is the supreme person. The impersonalists' understanding of

God is called *nirarcā*. *Niḥ* means "negative" and *arcā* means "form," so *nirarcā* means "negative form." The impersonalists are mistaken when they think that God has no form at all. The word *nirarcā* does not indicate that He has no form, but that he has no material form as we do. Form is there, but it is not material; it is spiritual form.

What is the value of our form? This form will be changed after a few years, as soon as we give up the body. Our forms are changed just as we change our suits and dresses, but God doesn't have a form like this; therefore He is sometimes called *nirarcā*. Form is there, and that also has been explained in the *Brahma-saṁhitā*. Lord Brahmā describes His form in this way:

veṇuṁ kvaṇantam aravinda-dalāyatākṣaṁ
barhāvataṁsam asitāmbuda-sundarāṅgam
kandarpa-koṭi-kamanīya-viśeṣa-śobhaṁ
govindam ādi-puruṣaṁ tam ahaṁ bhajāmi

aṅgāni yasya sakalendriya-vṛttimanti
paśyanti pānti kalayanti ciraṁ jaganti
ānanda-cinmaya-sad-ujjvala-vigrahasya
govindam ādi-puruṣaṁ tam ahaṁ bhajāmi

"I worship Govinda, the primeval Lord, who is adept at playing on His flute, with blooming eyes like lotus petals, with head bedecked with a peacock's feather, with the figure of beauty tinged with the hue of blue clouds, and His unique loveliness charming millions of Cupids. I worship Govinda, the primeval Lord, whose transcendental form is full of bliss, truth and substantiality and is thus full of the most dazzling splendor. Each of the limbs of that transcendental figure possesses, in Himself, the full-fledged functions of all the organs, and eternally sees, maintains and manifests the infinite universes, both spiritual and mundane." (*Bs.* 5.30,32)

This form has nothing whatsoever to do with material forms. Impersonalists say, "Oh, you say Kṛṣṇa has a form. If so, how can you say that He is the Supreme? The impersonal Brahman is the Supreme, and the impersonal Brahman is formless." But we have information from *Bhagavad-gītā* that Kṛṣṇa is the source of the impersonal Brahman.

brahmaṇo hi pratiṣṭhāham
amṛtasyāvyayasya ca
śāśvatasya ca dharmasya
sukhasyaikāntikasya ca

"And I am the basis of the impersonal Brahman, which is immortal and imperishable, eternal, the constitutional position of ultimate happiness." (Bg. 14.27)

Kṛṣṇa certainly has form, but His form, as stated before, is *sac-cid-ānanda-vigraha,* eternal, full of bliss, and full of knowledge. The attributes of His transcendental body are summarized by Lord Brahmā in this way:

īśvaraḥ paramaḥ kṛṣṇaḥ
sac-cid-ānanda-vigrahaḥ

anādir ādir govindaḥ
sarva-kāraṇa-kāraṇam

"Kṛṣṇa, who is known as Govinda, is the Supreme Godhead. He has an eternal, blissful spiritual body. He is the origin of all. He has no other origin and He is the prime cause of all causes."(*Bs.* 5.1)

The word Govinda means "He who gives pleasure to the senses." We perceive pleasure through our senses, and therefore Kṛṣṇa, who is the reservoir of pleasure, is called Govinda. If we serve Kṛṣṇa with purified senses, we will begin to relish the pleasure of that supreme reservoir.

How can we describe God or understand His glories? It is not possible. God is unlimited. Regardless of our finite limitations, however, we can express our own feelings and say, "My God, my Lord." This will be accepted. Lord Caitanya Mahāprabhu teaches us to pray in this way:

ayi nandatanuja kiṅkaraṁ
patitaṁ māṁ viṣame bhavāmbudhau
kṛpayā tava pāda-paṅkaja-
sthita-dhūlīsadṛśaṁ vicintaya

"O son of Mahārāja Nanda, I am Your eternal servitor, and although I am so, somehow or other I have fallen in the ocean of birth and death. Please, therefore, pick me up from this ocean of death and fix me as one of the atoms at Your lotus feet." *(Śikṣāṣṭakam, 5)*

This should be the standard of prayer; we should

only want to be placed as one of the atoms at Kṛṣṇa's lotus feet to render service unto Him. Everyone is praying to God with some interest, but even if we pray to God, "Give me some money, give me some relief, a nice house, a nice wife, or nice food," that is also good. Yet this is not to the standard of Lord Caitanya Mahāprabhu's prayer. Our only prayer should be that the Lord enable us to serve Him birth after birth. Our prayer should be, "Dear Lord, You are so great that I want to engage in Your service. I have been serving all these rascals, and I am not satisfied. Now I have come to You. Please engage me in Your service." This is the last word in prayer. Some people complain that when they pray to God they do not feel His presence. We should know that this is due to our incapacities, not God's. There are two conceptions of presence–the physical conception and the vibrational conception. The physical conception is temporary, whereas the vibrational conception is eternal. When we enjoy or relish the vibration of Kṛṣṇa's teachings in *Bhagavad-gītā,* or when we chant Hare Kṛṣṇa, we should know that by those vibrations He is immediately present. He is absolute, and because of this His vibration is just as important as His physical presence. When we feel separation from Kṛṣṇa or the spiritual master, we should just try to remember their words of instructions, and we will no longer feel that separation. Such association with Kṛṣṇa and the spiritual master should be association by vibration, not physical presence. That is real association. We put so much stress on seeing, but when

Kṛṣṇa was present on this earth, so many people saw Him and did not realize that He is God; so what is the advantage of seeing? By seeing Kṛṣṇa, we will not understand Him, but by listening carefully to His teachings, we can come to the platform of understanding. We can touch Kṛṣṇa immediately by sound vibration; therefore we should give more stress to the sound vibration of Kṛṣṇa and of the spiritual master—then we'll feel happy and won't feel separation.

From *Śrīmad-Bhāgavatam* we understand that when Kṛṣṇa departed from this world, Arjuna was overwhelmed with sorrow, but when he began to remember the instructions of *Bhagavad-gītā,* he became pacified. Arjuna was Kṛṣṇa's constant friend, so when Kṛṣṇa went to His abode, Arjuna was overwhelmed, but just by remembering His teachings he got relief from the pains of separation. Thus whenever we feel separation, it is best to remember the teachings. The teachings of *Bhagavad-gītā* were imparted to Arjuna for his happiness and for the happiness of all men. This is indicated by Kṛṣṇa, at the beginning of the Tenth Chapter, when He says:

bhūya eva mahā-bāho
śṛṇu me paramaṁ vacaḥ
yat te 'haṁ prīyamāṇāya
vakṣyāmi hita-kāmyayā

"Again, O mighty-armed Arjuna, listen to My supreme word, which I shall impart to you for your benefit and which will give you great joy." (Bg. 10.1)

By hearing the words of Lord Kṛṣṇa and following them carefully, we will attain not only peace in the world, but the supreme peace *(paraṁ śāntim)*. All that is required is that we seek refuge in the lotus feet of Kṛṣṇa and render service unto Him by chanting His glories and pushing this Kṛṣṇa consciousness movement in every town and village of the world. It is Kṛṣṇa's promise that by such surrender peace and eternal life will come automatically.

tam eva śaraṇaṁ gaccha
sarva-bhāvena bhārata
tatprasādāt paraṁ śāntiṁ
sthānaṁ prāpsyasi śāśvatam

"O scion of Bharata, surrender unto Him in all respects, so that by His mercy you can have transcendental peace and the eternal abode." (Bg. 18.62)

5

Knowing Kṛṣṇa's Energies

For Kṛṣṇa there is no difference between material and spiritual energy. For Him, it is all the same. Sometimes electricity works for cooling purposes, and sometimes it works for heating purposes, but the energy generated from the electric powerhouse is all the same. Similarly, Kṛṣṇa's energy is always spiritual, but it is acting in different ways. In a town there may be a department of welfare and a department of police. In the eyes of the government both are the same, for both are subsidiary parts of the government, but for the individual they render different services. The material energy may be working in different ways that may not be very pleasant to the living entity, but that does not mean that material energy is not liked by Kṛṣṇa. It is as important as spiritual energy, but it is engaged to punish the conditioned soul, just as the police department is engaged in punishing criminals. In the *Brahma-saṁhitā,* it is confirmed that Kṛṣṇa's energy is always spiritual, but it is acting in different ways in different fields of activities. In relation to Kṛṣṇa there is no distinction between the energies, but for our understanding we discriminate and say that sometimes the energy is working in a material way and sometimes in a spiritual way. We are thinking that the energy is hot or cold, good or bad, pleasant or unpleasant, but in fact the energy is the same.

Kṛṣṇa cannot distribute inferior energy because He is not inferior. He is always superior, spiritual, and therefore His energy is always spiritual. Subhadrā is the sister of Kṛṣṇa, and from her comes the incarnation of Durgā, the personification of material energy. Subhadrā is in the spiritual world and is eternally related to Kṛṣṇa as His energy, but when Durgā conducts her activities here in the material world, it is not that she is to be considered inferior. In the *Bhagavad-gītā* as well as in *Brahma-saṁhitā* it is said that Durgā or Māyā is acting under Kṛṣṇa's direction, so how can she be considered inferior? Criminals may think that the police department is an inferior governmental department, but the law-abiding citizens do not think that this is so. It simply functions in a particular way. Similarly, the material energy has to act to bewilder the living entity who is under the direction of Kṛṣṇa.

We are the living entities within the material energy, and we are in this position because we wanted to dominate material nature. Kṛṣṇa has given us the facility, saying, "All right, you may try, but you cannot be successful." As long as we are in ignorance of how the laws of nature are working under the supreme direction of Kṛṣṇa, we will continue to be defeated in our activities. When we understand Kṛṣṇa in perfection, we will automatically know the laws of nature and how they are acting. Vaiṣṇavas are concerned with the background of the laws of material nature. When we understand Kṛṣṇa in perfection, we can understand that there is in actuality no inferior or material energy, but that everything is spiritual. We can understand that on the higher platform whatever we are experiencing are the actions and reactions of the different energies of the Supreme Lord. When we understand Kṛṣṇa perfectly, then these distinctions of superior and inferior energies will disappear. Whatever is engaged in the service of Kṛṣṇa is superior energy. In the higher sense, everything is serving Kṛṣṇa, and those who are highly elevated understand this.

That the Lord has various energies is confirmed in Vedic literatures. Yet the Supreme Lord personally has nothing to do. How is this? He has not to strive for wealth, for all wealth is His; nor for knowledge, for all knowledge is His; nor for power, for all power is His; nor for beauty, fame or renunciation, for they are all His in full. Nor does He directly manage universal affairs, for He has many assistants who can conduct affairs while He remains in His abode. This is confirmed in *Śrī Īśopaniṣad:*

anejad ekaṁ manaso javīyo
nainad devā āpnuvan pūrvam arṣat
tad dhāvato'nyān atyeti tiṣṭhat
tasminn apo mātariśvā dadhāti

"The Personality of Godhead, although fixed in His abode, is more swift than the mind, and can overcome all others running. The powerful demigods cannot approach Him. Although in one place, He has control over those who supply the air and rain. He surpasses all in excellence." *(Śrī Īśopaniṣad, Mantra 4)*

Thus Kṛṣṇa has no work to perform. As the Supreme Personality of Godhead, He simply engages in enjoying Himself with the *gopīs* (cowherd girls) and His consort Rādhārāṇī. Kṛṣṇa, as Kṛṣṇa, does not really engage in killing demons. When Kṛṣṇa kills demons, He is known as Vāsudeva Kṛṣṇa, not the original Kṛṣṇa. When Kṛṣṇa expands Himself, He first expands as Balarāma, then Saṅkarṣaṇa, Pradyumna, Aniruddha and Vāsudeva. As Vāsudeva, He acts in Mathurā and Dvārakā, but as Kṛṣṇa, in His original feature, He remains in Vṛndāvana. This may seem to be confusing; even one of the greatest fiction writers in Bengal misunderstood and thought that Kṛṣṇa of Vṛndāvana, Kṛṣṇa of Dvārakā, and Kṛṣṇa of Mathurā were three different persons. But this is not difficult to understand if we know the nature of Kṛṣṇa's expansions. Kṛṣṇa is the same, and He is the one without a second, but He can expand Himself in billions and trillions of forms. This is all for the purpose of His enjoyment.

In the Tenth Chapter of *Bhagavad-gītā*, Kṛṣṇa explains His different manifestations to Arjuna in this way:

uccaiḥśravasam aśvānāṁ
viddhi māṁ amṛtodbhavam
airāvataṁ gajendrāṇāṁ
narāṇāṁ ca narādhipam

āyudhānām ahaṁ vajraṁ
dhenūnām asmi kāmadhuk
prajanaś cāsmi kandarpaḥ
sarpāṇām asmi vāsukiḥ

"Of horses know Me to be Uccaiḥśravā, who rose out of the ocean, born of the elixir of immortality; of lordly elephants I am Airāvata, and among men I am the monarch. Of weapons I am the thunderbolt; among cows I am Kāmadhuk, giver of abundant milk. Of procreators I am Kandarpa, the god of love; and of serpents I am Vāsuki, the chief." (Bg. 10.27,28)

Lord Kṛṣṇa further enumerated the many great manifestations of the material creation and explained how each was representative of Himself. He concluded a long detailed account of these manifestations by saying:

athavā bahunaitena
kiṁ jñātena tavārjuna
viṣṭabhyāham idaṁ kṛtsnam
ekāṁśena sthito jagat

"But what need is there, Arjuna, for all this detailed knowledge? With a single fragment of Myself I pervade and support these entire universes." (Bg. 10.42)

Thus this material world is existing on one plenary portion of Kṛṣṇa. If Kṛṣṇa didn't enter this universe, it could not exist. Similarly, unless the spirit soul, which is a fragmental portion of Kṛṣṇa, enters this body, this body cannot exist. As soon as the spirit soul leaves, the body immediately becomes useless; when Kṛṣṇa enters into matter, matter has value. This is true for the minute individual atom and the great universe as well.

Since the manifestations of Kṛṣṇa are so great, we should know that His enjoyment is far greater than ours. We have to try to understand what kind of enjoyment Kṛṣṇa likes. Everyone knows that God is great, and we can conclude from this that His enjoyment is great also. In this regard, Svarūpa Dāmodara Gosvāmī has written a verse which says that although the loving affairs of Rādhā and Kṛṣṇa may appear like ordinary material affairs, this is not actually the case. Rādhārāṇī is the pleasure potency of Kṛṣṇa. In the *Vedānta-sūtra* the Absolute Truth is said to be always enjoying the pleasure potency. When we want pleasure, we cannot have it alone. We feel pleasure in the company of friends or family. I may speak in a room alone, but if I speak in a room before other people, the pleasure is increased. Pleasure means that there must be others, and therefore Kṛṣṇa, the Absolute Truth, who is always engaged in enjoying Himself, has become many.

We are Kṛṣṇa's parts and parcels and have been created to give pleasure to Kṛṣṇa. The chief pleasure potency is Rādhārāṇi, and so Rādhā-Kṛṣṇa are always together. Whereas the material energy is conducted by the external potency, Māyā, the spiritual world is conducted by the internal potency, Rādhārāṇī. We often pray to Rādhārāṇī because She is the pleasure potency of Kṛṣṇa. The very word "Kṛṣṇa" means all-attractive, but Rādhārāṇī is so great that She attracts Kṛṣṇa. If Kṛṣṇa is always attractive to everyone, and Rādhārāṇī is attractive to Kṛṣṇa, how can we imagine the position of Śrīmatī Rādhārāṇī? We should try humbly to understand and offer Her our obeisances, saying, "Rādhārāṇī, You are so dear to Kṛṣṇa. You are the daughter of King Vṛṣabhānu, and

You are Kṛṣṇa's beloved. We offer our respectful obeisances unto You." Rādhārāṇī is very dear to Kṛṣṇa, and if we approach Kṛṣṇa through the mercy of Rādhārāṇī, we can easily attain Him. If Rādhārāṇī recommends a devotee, Kṛṣṇa immediately accepts him, however foolish he may be. Consequently in Vṛndāvana we find that devotees chant Rādhārāṇī's name more often than Kṛṣṇa's. Wherever we go in India we will find devotees calling, "Jaya Rādhe." We should be more interested in worshiping Rādhārāṇī, for however fallen we may be, if somehow or other we can please Her, we can very easily understand Kṛṣṇa. If we try to understand Kṛṣṇa by the speculative process, we will have to spend many lifetimes of speculation; but if we take to devotional service and just try to please Rādhārāṇī, then Kṛṣṇa can be very easily realized. Rādhārāṇī is such a great devotee that She can deliver Kṛṣṇa.

Even Kṛṣṇa cannot understand Rādhārāṇī's qualities. He fails to understand Her because She is so great. In order to understand Rādhārāṇī, Kṛṣṇa actually accepted Her position. Kṛṣṇa thought, "Although I am full and complete in every respect, I still don't understand Rādhārāṇī. Why is that?" This obliged Kṛṣṇa to accept the propensities of Rādhārāṇī, and this accounts for His manifestation as Lord Caitanya Mahāprabhu. Caitanya Mahāprabhu is Kṛṣṇa Himself, but He is Kṛṣṇa accepting the propensities of Rādhārāṇī. Rādhārāṇī is always feeling separation from Kṛṣṇa, and similarly, in the position of Rādhārāṇī, Lord Caitanya was always feeling that separation. Furthermore, those who follow the teachings of Lord Caitanya should experience and relish the feelings of separation, not of meeting.

The *gosvāmīs,* disciples of Lord Caitanya Mahāprabhu, the most perfect and highly elevated beings, never said, "I have seen Kṛṣṇa." Instead, they constantly cried, "Where is Rādhārāṇī? Where are Lalitā and Viśākhā and the other damsels of Vṛndāvana?" In their mature stage of love of Godhead, when they were living in Vṛndāvana, the *gosvāmīs* would also cry, "Rādhārāṇī, where are You? Where are Your associates? Where are You, O son of Nanda Mahārāja? Where are you all?" In this way they were searching after Kṛṣṇa, and they never at any time said, "Last night I saw Kṛṣṇa dancing with the *gopīs.*" Such claims are not made by a mature devotee, but by one who takes things very cheaply. Some people think that Rādhā and Kṛṣṇa are so cheap that They may be seen every night, but this is not the teaching of the *gosvāmīs* who were always searching after Kṛṣṇa crying, "Where are You? Where are You Rādhārāṇī? Where are You Kṛṣṇa? Are You there by Govardhana Hill? Are You on the bank of the Yamunā?" In this way, throughout the whole tract of Vṛndāvana, the *gosvāmīs* were crying and searching after Rādhā and Kṛṣṇa like madmen.

We have to follow in the footprints of the *gosvāmīs* and search out Rādhā and Kṛṣṇa in this way. Vṛndāvana is in our hearts, and we must search for Him there. This is the process recommended by Caitanya Mahāprabhu, the process of worship in separation. Feeling separation from Kṛṣṇa, Lord Caitanya Mahāprabhu would throw Himself into the sea. Sometimes He would leave His room in the dead of night and disappear. No one would know where He had gone, but all the while He was searching after Kṛṣṇa. Thus it is not that we are to enjoy the loving exchanges between Kṛṣṇa and Rādhā like spectators at some sports show. We must feel separation from Them. The more we feel separation, the more we should understand that we are advancing. With our material senses, we cannot see Kṛṣṇa, nor can we even hear His name. We can begin to perceive Him when we advance in devotional service. That devotional service begins with the tongue, not the legs, eyes or ears. The tongue must be utilized to chant Hare Kṛṣṇa, Hare Kṛṣṇa, Kṛṣṇa Kṛṣṇa, Hare Hare/ Hare Rāma, Hare Rāma, Rāma Rāma, Hare Hare and take Kṛṣṇa *prasādam.* Thus the tongue has a dual function, and by utilizing it in this way, we will realize Kṛṣṇa. We cannot see Kṛṣṇa with our material eyes, nor hear about Him with material ears, nor touch Him with our hands; but if we engage our tongue in His service, He will reveal Himself, saying, "Here I am."

This chanting of Hare Kṛṣṇa extinguishes the blazing fire of material nature. This is also the purport to the following prayer to the spiritual master.

saṁsāra-dāvānala-līḍha-loka
trāṇāya kāruṇya-ghanāghanatvam
prāptasya kalyāṇa-guṇārṇavasya
vande guroḥ śrī-caraṇāravindam

"The spiritual master is receiving benediction from the ocean of mercy. Just as the cloud pours water on the forest fire to extinguish it, so the spiritual master extinguishes the blazing fire of material existence. I offer my respectful obeisances unto the lotus feet of my spiritual master." (*Śrī Gurvaṣṭakam,* Verse 1)

This material world is often compared to a forest fire which takes place automatically. No one wants a forest fire, but there is often lightning, or carelessness, or friction, or whatever, and the fire immediately takes place. Similarly, this material world is beset with a blazing fire of problems. Everyone wants to live here peacefully, but situations develop in such a way that this is not possible for anyone. We struggle very hard to adjust things in so many ways, but nature's laws are so cruel and dangerous that in spite of our hopes and plans the blazing fire of the problems of material existence continues.

In this century, for instance, we have attempted to put out the fire of war, but it has not been possible. There was a First World War, and then a League of Nations was formed to try to prevent a second, but despite their attempts a second took place. Now a United Nations has been constructed to help end war, but war is going on in Viet Nam, in Egypt, in Pakistan and other places. No one wants a Third World War, but it seems imminent. It is not possible to send a fire brigade, a few men with buckets of water, to extinguish a great fire in the forest. To extinguish a roaring forest fire there must be volumes of water; in other words, there must be an arrangement that is beyond human endeavor. When there is a merciful cloud over the forest fire, the cloud bursts, rain pours down in torrents, and the blazing fire is immediately extinguished. As a cloud collects water from the ocean, similarly the spiritual master collects water from Kṛṣṇa's ocean of mercy and pours it over the blazing fire of material existence. Thus one who bestows or distributes the merciful rain of Kṛṣṇa is called a spiritual master or *guru.*

In Vedic literatures it is said that in order to understand the transcendental science of Kṛṣṇa consciousness, we must try to acquire knowledge of how to extinguish this blazing fire of problems. Scientists, philosophers and other educated men are trying very hard to extinguish it, but the result seems to be bigger and bigger bombs. The *karmīs* or fruitive laborers are working with heart and soul, day and night, to extinguish this fire or to diminish the miserable condition of material existence by dint of hard labor. The *jñānīs* or philosophers are also trying, but they have become disgusted and so proclaim, "This world is false." Thinking this, they try to merge into the existence of the Supreme and in this way extinguish the fire. This is like the jackel who tries to pick some grapes from a vine, and when he fails, says, "Oh, these grapes are sour anyway." The *yogīs* or meditators try to gain superior mystic power by becoming greater than the greatest, smaller than the smallest, lighter than the lightest, and heavier than the heaviest, but this is just so much child's play. With any material body—whether it be great or small, light or heavy—the problems of material existence still remain. In this way one may progress from one stage to another, coming from the stage of *karmī* or fruitive laborer, to the stage of *jñānī* or philosopher, to the stage of *yogī* or meditator, but in any case one finally has to come to the platform of *bhakti,* or devotional service. This is the real evolutionary process. It is indicated in *Bhagavad-gītā* in this way:

bahūnāṁ janmanām ante
jñānavān māṁ prapadyate
vāsudevaḥ sarvam iti
sa mahātmā sudurlabhaḥ

"After many births and deaths, he who is actually in knowledge surrenders unto Me, knowing Me to be the cause of all causes, and all that is. Such a great soul is very rare." (Bg. 7.19)

Surrender to Kṛṣṇa is the point; that is the aim of life, and the *bhaktas,* the intelligent men of the world, take to this stage immediately. Therefore Kṛṣṇa says that they are wise men. If, after many, many births one has to come to this point of surrender, then why not immediately?

The blazing fire of material nature is supervised by Durgā. Often she is portrayed with weapons in her hands. She has ten hands, and each holds a different type of weapon. This indicates that she is ruling all ten directions of this universe. She wields the different weapons to chastise the demons. There is one famous picture of a demon struggling with a lion, and the goddess Durgā is pulling the demon's hair and pushing her trident against his chest. If we study this picture we can determine that we are the demon and that the trident is the threefold miseries of material existence from which we are always suffering. Some miseries are inflicted by other living entities, some are inflicted by natural disasters, and some are inflicted by the mind and body themselves. In one way or another we are always struggling against these three types of miseries. No one in the material creation can say that he is free from them. The trident of this material nature is pressed against everyone's chest, and because of this, pure happiness within this material world is not possible. We may try to satisfy Mother Durgā by worshiping her or by giving her some bribe, but Durgā is not so easily bribed.

Therefore we should know that our aim of life should be to understand the Supreme Personality of Godhead. We should make every arrangement—social, political, philosophical or religious—but the aim should be to approach the Supreme Person. In the *Vedas* it is stated that the learned advanced people, the demigods of the creation, simply look to the lotus feet of Kṛṣṇa. The aim should be the same with human civilization. Without looking to Kṛṣṇa's lotus feet, all religious, social or political endeavors will fail. It is not possible to make progress as long as our desires are anchored in the material world. In this regard, there is a story of a bridegroom's party who had to go to the bride's house down the river. It was settled that they would start at night by boat and reach the destination early in the morning. Therefore at night, after supper, the jubilant party got aboard a boat, made themselves comfortable and instructed the boatmen to start.

Since all the members of the party were seated comfortably, and since the river breeze was very pleasant, they slept soundly that night. In the morning they all got up early, but to their astonishment they saw that the boat had not moved an inch toward the destination, even though the boatmen had rowed vigorously all night long. Finally, after inquiring, they found that despite the boatmen's rowing, the boat had not moved because they had failed to raise the anchor. The marriage ceremony was thus spoiled because of a foolish mistake.

Our present civilization is therefore a mistaken civilization because the mistaken leaders have forgotten to raise the anchor of attachment. Instead, the anchor is being more and more firmly fixed because they have structured the social order on the basis of sense gratification. This sense gratifying social and political set-up, maintained by various plans and schemes, has been described in *Bhagavad-gītā* as follows:

kāmam āśritya duṣpūraṁ
dambha-māna-madānvitāḥ
mohād gṛhītvāsad-grāhān
pravartante 'śuci-vratāḥ

cintām aparimeyāṁ ca
pralayāntām upāśritāḥ
kāmopabhoga-paramā
etāvad iti niścitāḥ

"The demoniac, taking shelter of insatiable lust, pride, and false prestige, and being thus illusioned, are always sworn to unclean work, attracted by the impermanent. Their belief is that to gratify the senses unto the end of life is the prime necessity of human civilization. Thus, there is no measurement for their anxiety." (Bg. 16.10-11)

The leaders, like the boatmen, are all illusioned. They mislead us into taking some temporary benefit, but how long can their plans and schemes go on? If they persist until they die of heart failure or are killed by assassins, then another just like them takes their place. Even the so-called philosophers of modern society are captivated by material name and fame, and so they do not lead the general populace in the proper direction. Thus the anchor of life remains deeply fixed in the waters of nescience for the purpose of sense gratification, and thus our so-called civilization rots in a stagnant pool. Because we are not moving, we are always in the same port of problematic life. All schemes are only useless scraps of paper in the face of war, famine, earthquakes and other disasters. All these disasters are warnings from Mother Durgā, and by them she confirms her eternal superiority over the illusioned planmakers. The different weights on the anchor which keep us grounded in material life are our attachments to the material body due to our ignorance of spiritual facts, our attachment to kinsmen due to bodily relations, our attachment to our land of birth and our material possessions, our attachment to material science and our attachment to religious forms and rituals without knowing their true purpose—all these anchor the boat of the human body in the material universe.

Śrī Kṛṣṇa, using the example of a strongly rooted banyan tree, advises us in *Bhagavad-gītā* how to get rid of this attachment once and for all:

na rūpam asyeha tathopalabhyate
nānto na cādir na ca sampratiṣṭhā
aśvattham enaṁ suvirūḍha-mūlam
asaṅga-śastreṇa dṛḍhena chittvā

tataḥ padaṁ tat parimārgitavyaṁ
yasmin gatā na nivartanti bhūyaḥ
tam eva cādyaṁ puruṣaṁ prapadye
yataḥ pravṛttiḥ prasṛtā purāṇī

"The real form of this tree cannot be perceived in this world. No one can understand where it ends, where it begins, or where its foundation is. This banyan tree must be cut out with determination, by the weapon of detachment. Thereafter, one must seek that situation from which, having gone, one never comes back. One must surrender to that Supreme Personality of Godhead from whom everything has begun and is extending since time immemorial." (Bg. 15.3,4)

The Personality of Godhead, who is fully cognizant of everything in His creation, informs us in our best interest that we must desire to get rid of this material existence. We must detach ourselves from everything material. To make the best use of a bad bargain, our material existence should be 100% spiritualized by constant association with Kṛṣṇa's message, His devotees and His names. Therefore everyone who ordinarily engages in material affairs can derive the highest benefit from this Kṛṣṇa consciousness movement. All kinds of spiritual endeavors are more or less tinged with material contamination. However, pure devotional service is transcendental to all pollution. We need not artificially adopt principles of materialism; we need only fix our minds on the lotus feet of the Supreme Lord, the Personality of Godhead, Śrī Kṛṣṇa.

6
Taking to Kṛṣṇa Consciousness

In India all scriptures and great spiritual teachers, including Śaṅkarācārya, an impersonalist, accept Kṛṣṇa as the Supreme Lord. In the beginning of his commentary on the *Bhagavad-gītā*, Śaṅkarācārya says that Nārāyaṇa is transcendental to this manifested and unmanifested creation, and in the same commentary he says that the Supreme Personality of Godhead, Nārāyaṇa, is Kṛṣṇa appearing as the son of Devakī and Vasudeva. Thus in this respect there is little difference of opinion about Kṛṣṇa. Those who are authorities, be they personalists or impersonalists, are in agreement that Kṛṣṇa is the Supreme Lord.

When Kṛṣṇa was present on this planet, He proved by His activities and opulence that He is the Supreme Lord. If we are actually anxious to understand who and what the Supreme Lord is, all of the information is given in Vedic literatures. If we utilize whatever we have in our possession to understand God, Kṛṣṇa will prove that He is the Supreme Personality of Godhead. If we but accept this one fact, then all of our education is complete. It is fashionable to research to try to find out who is God, but this is not necessary. God is present, and He Himself says:

mattaḥ parataraṁ nānyat
kiñcid asti dhanañjaya
mayi sarvam idaṁ protaṁ
sūtre maṇi-gaṇā iva

"O conqueror of wealth (Arjuna), there is no truth superior to Me. Everything rests upon Me, as pearls are strung on a thread." (Bg. 7.7)

This information is not only given in *Bhagavad-gītā* but in other scriptures as well, and it has been accepted from the very beginning by great *ācāryas* (teachers) like Śaṅkarācārya, Rāmānujācārya, Madhvācārya, Lord Caitanya and many other stalwart authorities. Even at the present moment those who do not accept Kṛṣṇa as the Supreme Lord are accepting the knowledge given by Kṛṣṇa to Arjuna. So in this way they are accepting Kṛṣṇa indirectly. If one accepts *Bhagavad-gītā* as a great book of knowledge, he is also accepting Kṛṣṇa. There is no doubt that the Supreme Absolute Truth is Kṛṣṇa and that we have our eternal relationship with Him.

Our eternal relationship with God is *sabhājana:* God is great, and we are subordinate. He is the predominator, and we are the predominated. The duty of the subordinate is to please the predominator. Similarly, if we want to be happy, we must learn how to make Kṛṣṇa happy. This is the process of Kṛṣṇa consciousness.

But how is it to be understood that the Supreme Lord is satisfied by our service and labor? It is actually possible to perfect our service or occupational duty. Everyone has some service to perform according to his designations. He may be an Indian or American, Hindu, Muslim or Christian, man, woman, *brāhmaṇa, kṣatriya, vaiśya, śūdra* or whatever—in any case he is meant to do some sort of work, and that work is his occupational duty.

Perfection of duty can be tested by seeing whether the Supreme Lord is satisfied by its execution. The Supreme Lord's satisfaction can be tested by the Lord's representative, the spiritual master. Therefore it is important to seek out a real representative of the Supreme Personality of Godhead and work under him. If he is satisfied, then we should know that the Supreme Lord is also satisfied. That is explained by Viśvanātha Cakravartī Ṭhākura:

yasya prasādād bhagavat-prasādo
yasyāprasādān na gatiḥ kuto'pi
dhyāyaṁ stuvaṁs tasya yaśas tri-sandhyaṁ
vande guroḥ śrī-caraṇāravindam

"By the mercy of the spiritual master one is benedicted by the mercy of Kṛṣṇa. Without the grace of the spiritual master no one can make any advancement. Therefore I should always remember the spiritual master. At least three times a day I should offer my respectful obeisances unto the lotus feet of my spiritual master." (*Śrī Gurvaṣṭakam,* Verse 8)

The spiritual master is the representative of the Supreme Lord. How does he become the representative? If one says that such and such an object is a pair of spectacles, and if he teaches his disciple in that way, there is no mistake as to the identity of the object. The spiritual master is he who has captured the words of a particular disciplic succession. In the case given, the key word is "spectacles"—that's all. The spiritual master does not have to say anything beyond that. This is the qualification.

Kṛṣṇa says, "I am the Supreme," and the spiritual master says, "Kṛṣṇa is the Supreme." It is not that to be a representative of Kṛṣṇa or to be a spiritual master one has to have any extraordinary qualification. He simply has to carry the message from the authority as it is without any personal interpretation. As soon as there is some personal interpretation, the message is lost and the instructions become offensive. A person who interprets the scriptures according to his own whims should be immediately rejected.

Once Lord Caitanya Mahāprabhu said, "You must at least have enough sense to test to find out who is a spiritual master and who is not." For instance, if we want to purchase something, we must at least have some idea of what that thing is, otherwise we will be cheated. If we want to purchase a mango from the market, we must at least know what type of food a mango is and what it looks like. Similarly, we must have some preliminary knowledge of the qualifications for a bona fide spiritual master. *Bhagavad-gītā* itself gives some information about the succession of spiritual masters. Lord Śrī Kṛṣṇa says:

imaṁ vivasvate yogaṁ
proktavān aham avyayam
vivasvān manave prāha
manur ikṣvākave 'bravīt

evaṁ paramparā-prāptam
imaṁ rājarṣayo viduḥ

sa kāleneha mahatā
yogo naṣṭaḥ parantapa

sa evāyaṁ mayā te 'dya
yogaḥ proktaḥ purātanaḥ
bhakto 'si me sakhā ceti
rahasyaṁ hy etad uttamam

"I instructed this imperishable science of *yoga* to the sun-god Vivasvān, and Vivasvān instructed it to Manu, the father of mankind, and Manu in turn instructed it to Ikṣvāku. This supreme science was thus received through the chain of disciplic succession, and the saintly kings understood it in that way. But in course of time the succession was broken, and therefore the science as it is appears to be lost. That very ancient science of the relationship with the Supreme is today told by Me to you because you are My devotee as well as My friend; therefore, you can understand the transcendental mystery of this science." (Bg. 4.1-3)

That original spiritual disciplic succession was broken, but now we can receive the same message by studying *Bhagavad-gītā*. In *Bhagavad-gītā* Kṛṣṇa speaks to Arjuna just as in a far distant time He spoke to the sun-god. If we accept the words of Arjuna and Kṛṣṇa, it may be possible for us to understand *Bhagavad-gītā*, but if we want to interpret it in our own way, the results will be nonsensical. The best way to understand *Bhagavad-gītā* is to accept a bona fide spiritual master. This is not very difficult.

Arjuna says that he accepts all that Kṛṣṇa has said to him because Kṛṣṇa is the Supreme Personality of Godhead:

naṣṭo mohaḥ smṛtir labdhā
tvat prasādān mayācyuta
sthito'smi gata-sandehaḥ
kariṣye vacanaṁ tava

"Arjuna said, My dear Kṛṣṇa, O infallible one, my illusion is now gone. I have regained my memory by Your mercy, and now I am fixed without any doubt, prepared to act according to Your instructions." (Bg. 18.73)

As Arjuna, we should accept Kṛṣṇa as the Supreme Personality of Godhead and do as He says:

yat karoṣi yad aśnāsi
yaj juhoṣi dadāsi yat
yat tapasyasi kaunteya
tat kuruṣva madarpanam

"O son of Kuntī, all that you do, all that you eat, all that you offer and give away, as well as all austerities that you may perform, should be done as an offering unto Me." (Bg. 9.27)

By accepting Kṛṣṇa in this spirit, we can attain complete knowledge. If, however, we do not accept Kṛṣṇa and interpret *Bhagavad-gītā* in our own way, then everything will be spoiled.

If we are sincere, we will get a sincere spiritual master by the grace of Kṛṣṇa. If, however, we want to be cheated, Kṛṣṇa will send us a cheater, and we will be cheated throughout our lives. That is actually going on. For those who do not want to understand Kṛṣṇa as He is but want to understand by dint of their own imperfect vision, Kṛṣṇa, God, remains unknown.

The whole process is to accept Kṛṣṇa and His instructions and therefore to render devotional service unto Him. It is Śrīmatī Rādhārāṇī who is the very embodiment of perfect devotional service. In the *Brahma-saṁhitā* Rādhārāṇī is described as Kṛṣṇa's expansion of His spiritual potency. In this way, She is nondifferent from Kṛṣṇa. The *gopīs,* who tend Rādhā and Kṛṣṇa, are not ordinary women or girls; they are expansions of Kṛṣṇa's pleasure potency. Rādhārāṇī and the *gopīs* should never be accepted as ordinary women; indeed, to understand their position we need the guidance of a spiritual master. If we living entities want to actually associate with Rādhārāṇī, that may be possible, although She is not an ordinary woman. We can become associates of Rādhārāṇī by qualifying ourselves in advanced devotional service.

In devotional service there is no frustration; even if we perform only a small amount, it will grow. Devotional service is never lost. As far as material things are concerned, whatever we gain in the world will be lost when the body is finished. But since we are eternal spiritual sparks, our spiritual assets go with us, gradually fructifying. In this way those who have previously cultivated transcendental consciousness come in contact with Kṛṣṇa consciousness through this movement. Interest in Kṛṣṇa consciousness is not commonplace. In *Bhagavad-gītā* it is said that out of many millions and billions of persons, only one is interested in achieving perfection. If we can advertise that simply by reading this book and meditating for fifteen minutes anyone can immediately get power, become successful in business and pass his examination, many people would be attracted to the book. People are not attracted to Kṛṣṇa consciousness because they prefer to be cheated by *māyā.* They think that the perfection of life is in eating a great supply of food, or in sleeping twenty hours, or in having a new mate every night or every day. People are interested in these things, but not in the perfection of life.

Every intelligent man should at least experiment with Kṛṣṇa consciousness. He should say, "All right. I have been enjoying this eating and sleeping for so many lives. These things were available for me to enjoy in my bird and animal bodies. Now in this life let me restrict the four principles of animalistic life–eating, sleeping, defending and mating–and let me devote my time to developing Kṛṣṇa consciousness. In this way my life will be successful."

It is not that we have coined this term "Kṛṣṇa consciousness." Kṛṣṇa consciousness is the oldest phrase in the history of the world:

man-manā bhava mad-bhakto
mad-yājī māṁ namaskuru
mām evaiṣyasi satyaṁ te
pratijāne priyo 'si me

man-manā bhava mad-bhakto
mad-yājī māṁ namaskuru
mām evaiṣyasi yuktvaivam
ātmānaṁ matparāyaṇaḥ

"Always think of Me. Become My devotee. Worship Me, and offer your homage unto Me. The result is that you will come to Me without fail. I promise you this, because you are My very dear friend. Engage your mind always in thinking of Me, engage your body in My service; and surrender unto Me. Completely absorbed in Me, surely will you come to Me." (Bg. 18.65, 9.34)

The phrase *man-manā bhava mad-bhakto* means "just be always conscious of Me." This then is Kṛṣṇa consciousness. In *Bhagavad-gītā* Kṛṣṇa is repeatedly saying that we should worship Him, offer obeisances unto Him and then come to Him. *Bhagavad-gītā* clearly points to the absolute necessity of Kṛṣṇa consciousness, and *Bhagavad-gītā* is accepted as the essence of the *Upaniṣads.* Even from the historical point of view, it has no comparison. It has been calculated on the basis of archeological evidence that Kṛṣṇa spoke *Bhagavad-gītā* on the Battlefield of Kurukṣetra more than five thousand years ago. So this Kṛṣṇa consciousness movement, even from the historical point of view, is five thousand years old. Its philosophy is the oldest in the history of the world. If we wish to trace it even further back, we find that Śrī Kṛṣṇa spoke it earlier to the sun-god. Kṛṣṇa is eternal, and consciousness of Kṛṣṇa is also eternal. In this way Kṛṣṇa consciousness should be approached. It should not simply be considered a theory.

When Kṛṣṇa consciousness is covered by any other consciousness, we experience our contaminated conditional life. When the sky is clear, we can see the sun's brilliant effulgence, but when it is covered by clouds, we cannot see it. We may be able to perceive the sunlight, but we cannot see the sun disc itself. When the sky is clear, it is in its natural condition. Similarly, our consciousness is eternally Kṛṣṇa consciousness because we are part and parcel of Kṛṣṇa eternally. This is asserted in the Fifteenth Chapter of *Bhagavad-gītā:*

mamaivāṁśo jīva-loke
jīva-bhūtaḥ sanātanaḥ
manaḥ ṣaṣṭhānīndriyāṇi
prakṛti-sthāni karṣati

"The living entities in this conditional world are My fragmental parts, and they are eternal. But due to conditioned life, they are struggling very hard with the six senses, which include the mind." (Bg. 15.7)

Somehow or other we have come in contact with material nature, and because of the mind and the six senses, we are struggling hard to exist. That is Darwin's theory—the struggle for existence, survival of the fittest. However, the actual fact is that our constitutional position is not one of struggle. Struggle is the position of animal life. Human life should be blissful and should have as its goal spiritual advancement. At one time that was India's principle of life, and there was a class of people, the *brāhmaṇas,* who engaged themselves exclusively in spiritual culture. Although brahminical cultural life is enunciated in the scriptures of India, it is not for Indians alone, but for all human beings. The *Vedas* were written for all mankind, but it so happened that when the *Vedas* were written, what is now known as the Indian culture was the only one extant. At that time, the whole planet was called Bhāratavarṣa, after Emperor Bharata Mahārāja, the son of Ṛṣabhadeva. Bharata Mahārāja ruled the whole planet, but gradually the planet was divided up. So the *dharma* of Vedic culture should not simply be considered Indian or Hindu in a sectarian sense.

Often the word *dharma* is translated to mean religion, but to conceive of *dharma* as a religion is to misconceive the word. In general usage, the word religion refers to a particular type of faith. The word *dharma* does not. *Dharma* indicates the natural occupation of the living entity. For example, wherever there is fire, there is heat and light, so it may be said that heat and light are the *dharma* of fire. Fire cannot change its *dharma.* In the same way, liquidity is an intrinsic quality of water, and this quality cannot be changed. If it is, it can no longer be considered water. The *dharma* of the individual soul can never be changed, and that *dharma* is the occupational duty of rendering service unto the Supreme Lord. Faiths and religions can be changed. Today I may be a Hindu, but tomorrow I may become a Christian or Moslem. In this way faiths can be changed, but *dharma* is a natural sequence, a natural occupation or connection.

Kṛṣṇa says that as soon as there is a discrepancy in the discharge of the *dharmas* of the living entities, when there is an upsurge of unnatural activities, He descends. One of the principal purposes of His descent is to reestablish religious principles. The best system of religion is that which best trains us to surrender unto the Supreme Lord. This is the basic principle underlying *Bhagavad-gītā.* We can select our own religion and be Hindu, Moslem, Buddhist, Christian or whatever, as long as we know the real purpose of religion. Indeed, *Śrīmad-Bhāgavatam* does not recommend that we give up our present religion, but it does hint at the purpose of religion. That purpose is love of Godhead, and that religion which teaches us best how to love the Supreme Lord is the best religion.

In this age especially there is a general decay in the consciousness of the masses of people. A few people remember that there is a God, but for the most part people are forgetting Him. Therefore they cannot be happy. People are thinking that God is dead, or that we have no obligation to God, or that there is no God. This sort of thinking will never make for happiness. When civilization is godless or atheistic, as it is today, God or His representative comes to remind people of their relationship with the supreme consciousness.

When Sanātana Gosvāmī inquired from Lord Caitanya, "What am I? Why am I always in a miserable condition? What is the position of all living entities?" Śrī Caitanya Mahāprabhu immediately answered that the real identity is that of servant of God. We should not understand the word "servant" in the sense of materialistic servant. To become a servant of God is a great position. People are always trying to get some government post or some position in a reputed business firm because the service rendered in such positions earns great profits. Although we are very anxious to get good positions in the government service, we do not stop to think of getting a position in God's service. God is the government of all governments.

God's service is *dharma*. This *dharma* may be described differently in different countries according to different cultural and climatic conditions or situations, but in every religious scripture obedience to God is instructed. No scripture says that there is no God or that we as living entities are independent—not the Bible, the Koran, the *Vedas* or even the Buddhist literatures. Generally, according to Buddhist philosophy, there is no individual soul and no supreme soul, but actually since Lord Buddha is accepted by Vedic literatures as an incarnation of God, by obeying Lord Buddha one is actually following God. In the *Śrīmad-Bhāgavatam* there is a list of incarnations, and Lord Buddha is accepted as one of them. *Śrīmad-Bhāgavatam* was compiled by Vyāsadeva five thousand years ago, and Lord Buddha appeared about 2,600 years ago, so *Śrīmad-Bhāgavatam* actually foretold the event of his incarnation. Lord Buddha preached that there is no God and no soul, that this body is a combination of matter, and that when we dissolve this material combination, sensations of misery and happiness will no longer exist. Then Śaṅkarācārya appeared to preach that the external feature of Brahman, the body, is merely an illusion. In all religions, temple worship and acceptance of authority are present. We may accept Kṛṣṇa, or Lord Jesus Christ, or Jehovah, or Lord Buddha, or Śaṅkarācārya, or Guru Nanak, but in any case acceptance of authority is required.

In *Bhagavad-gītā* Lord Śrī Kṛṣṇa is accepted as the supreme authority. Sometimes Kṛṣṇa descends personally, and sometimes He descends by His incarnations. Sometimes He descends as sound vibration, and sometimes He descends as a devotee. There are many different categories of *avatāras*. In this present age Kṛṣṇa has descended in His holy name, Hare Kṛṣṇa, Hare Kṛṣṇa, Kṛṣṇa Kṛṣṇa, Hare Hare/ Hare Rāma, Hare Rāma, Rāma Rāma, Hare Hare. Lord Caitanya Mahāprabhu also confirmed that in this age of Kali, Kṛṣṇa has descended in the form of sound vibration. Sound is one of the forms which the Lord takes. Therefore it is stated that there is no difference between Kṛṣṇa and His name.

Today people have forgotten their relationship with God, but this incarnation of Kṛṣṇa in the form of His holy names, this chanting of Hare Kṛṣṇa, will deliver all the people of the world from their forgetfulness. Lord Caitanya Mahāprabhu says that if we chant or associate with the chanting of the holy names of Kṛṣṇa, we will reach the highest perfectional stage of life. According to *Śrīmad-Bhāgavatam* there are different processes for different ages, but the principle of each process remains valid in all ages. It is not that the chanting of Hare Kṛṣṇa is effective in this age and not in Satya-yuga. Nor is it that people were not chanting the holy names of Kṛṣṇa in Satya-yuga. In Satya-yuga meditation was the main process, and great *munis* meditated for periods extending upwards of 60,000 years. In this age, however, perfection by that means of meditation is not possible because we are so short-lived. Consequently in this age it is especially recommended that we all sit down together and chant Hare Kṛṣṇa. It is very easy, and everyone can take part in it. There is no necessity of education, nor are any previous qualifications required. In this age people are also very slow and unfortunate, and they are contaminated with bad association. Caitanya Mahāprabhu introduced the chanting of Hare Kṛṣṇa, Hare Kṛṣṇa, Kṛṣṇa Kṛṣṇa, Hare Hare/ Hare Rāma, Hare Rāma, Rāma Rāma, Hare Hare as a great means of propaganda for spreading love of God. It is not that it is recommended only for Kali-yuga. Actually, it is recommended for every age. There have always been many devotees who have chanted and reached perfection in all ages. That is the beauty of this Kṛṣṇa consciousness movement. It is not simply for one age, or for one country, or for one class of people. Hare Kṛṣṇa can be chanted by any man in any social position, in any country and in any age, for Kṛṣṇa is the Supreme Lord of all people in all social positions, in all countries, in all ages.

Please accept our Personal
Invitation for you to
come to the famous

Hare Krishna
Sunday Feast

and enjoy pure vegetarian
banquets, talks from
Bhagavad Gita, plays, films
and music.

Every Sunday
4.30pm

at your local
Hare Krishna Centre

(For addresses see last pages)

Glossary

Ānanda—spiritual bliss, pleasure.
Avatāra—an incarnation of God who descends from the spiritual world.

Bhagavad-gītā—the book which records the spiritual instructions given by Kṛṣṇa to His friend Arjuna on the Battlefield of Kurukṣetra.
Bhakti—devotional service to God.
Brāhmaṇas—the intellectual class in human society.

Cātur-varṇyam—divisions of labor in human society as described in the Vedic literatures.

Dharma—the natural occupation of the living entity, which is to serve God.

Gopīs—cowherd girl friends of Kṛṣṇa described in the Vedic literatures.
Govinda—Kṛṣṇa, who gives pleasure to the senses.
Guru—spiritual master.

Jagadīśa—the Lord of the universe, Kṛṣṇa.
Jīvas—living entities or souls.
Jñānīs—speculative philosophers.

Karma—fruitive activities or their reactions.
Karmīs—fruitive laborers.
Kṣatriyas—the administrative and military class in human society.
Kṣetrajña—the individual spirit soul who is the knower of the field of the body.

Līlā—transcendental pastimes of the Lord.
Līlā-puruṣottama—the Personality of Godhead, who is by His own nature always engaged in transcendental pastimes.

Mantra—a transcendental sound vibration.
Māyā—material atmosphere in which the conditioned soul tries to enjoy without God.

Nāras—living beings.

Prakṛti—material nature.

Sac-cid-ānanda-vigraha—description of God as a fully cognizant and eternally joyful personality with a full sense of His identity.
Śūdras—the common laborer class in human society.

Vaiśyas—the mercantile and agricultural class in human society.

INDEX

BOOKS by His Divine Grace A. C. Bhaktivedanta Swami Prabhupāda

Bhagavad-gītā As It Is
Śrīmad-Bhāgavatam, cantos 1–10 (30 vols.)
Kṛṣṇa, the Supreme Personality of Godhead (3 vols.)
Śrī Caitanya-caritāmṛta (17 vols.)
Teachings of Lord Caitanya
The Nectar of Devotion
The Nectar of Instruction
Śrī Īśopaniṣad
Easy Journey to Other Planets
Kṛṣṇa Consciousness: The Topmost Yoga System
Perfect Questions, Perfect Answers
Teachings of Lord Kapila, the Son of Devahūti
Transcendental Teachings of Prahlād Mahārāja
Teachings of Queen Kuntī
Kṛṣṇa, the Reservoir of Pleasure
The Science of Self-Realization
The Path of Perfection
Light of the Bhāgavata
Life Comes From Life
The Perfection of Yoga
Beyond Birth and Death
On the Way to Kṛṣṇa
Geetār-gān (Bengali)
Vairāgya-vidyā (Bengali)
Buddhi-yoga (Bengali)
Bhakti-ratna-bolī (Bengali)
Rāja-vidyā: The King of Knowledge
Elevation to Kṛṣṇa Consciousness
Kṛṣṇa Consciousness: The Matchless Gift
Back to Godhead magazine (founder)

A complete catalog is available upon request.
For your free copy, write to the address below.

Bhaktivedanta Book Trust
GPO Box 1477
Sydney, NSW 2001

CENTRES OF THE INTERNATIONAL SOCIETY FOR KRISHNA CONSCIOUSNESS

ISKCON is a world wide community of devotees of Krishna dedicated to the principles of bhakti-yoga. Classes are held in the evenings during the week, and a special feast and festival is held every Sunday afternoon. Write, call, or visit for further information.

GREAT BRITIAN AND IRELAND

Belfast, Northern Ireland—Brooklands, 140 Upper Dunmurray Lane/ (0232) 681328
Birmingham, West Midlands—84 Stanmore Rd., Edgebaston B16/ (021) 420 4999
Dublin, Eire—Hare Krishna Centre, 3 Temple Lane, Dublin 2/ (010) 353 1 6795887
Hare Krishan Island (Formally - Lake Island of Inish Rath)—Derrylin, County Fermanagh, Northern Ireland/ (03657) 21512
Leicester—21 Thorsby St., North Evington/ (0533) 737829
Liverpool—44 Rathbone Rd., L15 4HQ/ (051) 7342723
London, (city)—Sri Sri Radha Krishna Temple, 10 Soho St., W1V 5DA/ (071) 437-3622
London, (country)—Bhaktivedanta Manor for Vedic Studies, Letchmore Heath, Watford, Hertfordshire WD2 8EP/ (0923) 857244
Manchester—20 Mayfield Road, Whalley Range, M168FT/ (061) 2264416
Newcastle upon Tyne—Hare Krishna Centre, 21 Leazes Park Rd., / (091) 222 0150
Scotland—"Karuna Bhavan', Bankhouse Road, Lesmahagow, Lanarkshire ML11 9PT/ (0555) 894790

NORTH AMERICA

CANADA

Montreal, Quebec—1626 Pie IX Boulevard, H1V 2C5/ (514) 521-1301
Ottawa, Ontario—212 Somerset St., E., K1N 6V4/ (613) 233-18845
Regina, Saskatchewan—1279 Retallack St., S4T 2H8/ (306) 525 1640
Toronto, Ontario—243 Avenue Rd., M5R 2J6/ (416) 922-5415
Vancouver, B.C.—5462 S.E. Marine Dr., Burnaby, V5J 3G8/ (604) 433-9728

U.S.A.

Atlanta, Georgia—1287 Ponce de Leon Ave., N.E., 30306/ (404) 377-8680
Baltimore, Maryland—200 Bloomsbury Ave., Catonsville 21228/ (301) 744-9537
Berkeley, California—2334 Stuart St., 94705/ (415) 644-1113
Boston, Massachusetts—72 Commonwealth Ave., 02116/ (617) 247-8611
Carriere, Mississippi (New Talavan)—Route 2, Box 449, 39426/ (601) 798-8533
Chicago, Illinois—1716 W. Lunt Ave., 60626/ (312) 973-0900
Dallas, Texas—5430 Gurley Ave., 75223/ (214) 827-6330
Denver, Colorado—1400 Cherry St., 80220/ (303) 333-5461
Detroit, Michigan—383 Lennox Ave., 48215/ (313) 824-6000
Gainesville, Florida (New Raman-reti)—Box 819, Alachua, Florida 32615/ (904) 462-9046
Gainsville, Florida—214 N.W. 14th St., 32603/ (904) 336-4183
Gurabo, Puerto Rico—Rt. 181, Box 215-B, Bo.Sta. Rita, 00658/ (809) 737-5222
Hartford, Connecticut—1683 Main St., E. Hartford, 06108/ (203) 289-7252
Hillsbourough, North Carolina (New Gokula)—Rt.6, Box 701,27278/ (919) 732-6492

Honolulu, Hawaii—51 Coelho Way, 96817/ (808) 595-3947
Houston, Texas—1320 W. 34th. St., 77018/ (713) 686-4482
Laguna beach, California—285 Legion St., 92651/ (714) 494-7029
Lansing, Michigan—1914 E. Michigan Ave., 48912/ (517) 332-1823
Long Island, New York—197 S. Ocean Ave., Freeport, 11520/ (516) 378-6184
Los Angeles, California—3764 Watseka Ave., 90034/ (213) 836-2676
Miami Beach, Florida—3220 Virginia St., 33133/ (305) 442-7218
Mulberry, Tennessee (Murakri-sevaka)—Murari Project. Rt. No. 1., Box 146-, 37359/ (615) 759-7331
New Orleans, Louisiana—2936 Esplanade Ave., 70109/ (504) 488-7433
New York, New York—305 Schermerhorn St., Brooklyn, 11217/ (718) 855-6714
Philadelphia, Pennsylvania—51 W. Allens Lane, 19119/ (215) 247-4600
Philadelphia, Pennsylvania—529 South St., 19147/ (215) 238-1753
Port Royal, Pennsylvania (Gita-nagari)—R.D. No. 1, Box 839, 17082/ (717) 527-4101
San Diego, California—1030 Grand Ave., Pacific Beach, 92109/ (619) 483-2500
San Francisco, California—84 Carl st., 94117/ (415) 753-8647
Seattle, Washington—1420 228th Av., Issagvah, WA 98027/ (206) 391-3293
St. Louis, Missouri—3926 Lindell Blvd., 63108/ (314) 535-8085
Tallahassee, Florida—1323 Nylic St., 32304/ (904) 681-9258
Topanga, California—20395 Callon Dr., 90290/ (213) 455-1658
Towaco, New Jersey—(mail P.O. Box 109, 07082)/ (201) 299-0970
Walla Walla, Washington—314 E. Poplar, 99362/ (509) 529-9556
Washington, D.C.—10310 Oaklyn Dr., Potomac, Maryland 20854/ (301) 299-2100

AUSTRALIA

Adelaide —227 Henley Beach Rd., Torrensville. SA 5031. (08) 234-1378
Bambra — New Nandagram , 'Oak Hill' Dean's Marsh Road, Bambra, VIC 3241/ (052) 887383
Brisbane — 95 Bank Rd., Graceville, QLD 4075, (mail: PO Box 83, Indooroopilly, 4068)/ (07) 379-5455
Canberra — GPO Box 1411, Canberra. ACT. 2601 /(062) 290-1869
Cessnock---New Gokula Farm, Lewis Lane,off Mountain View Rd, Millfield, via Cessnock. NSW 2325. (049) 981-800
Melbourne — 197 Danks St., Albert Park, VIC 3206, (mail: PO Box 125, Albert Park, VIC 3206)/ (03) 699-5122
Murwillumbah — New Govardhana , Tyalgum Rd., Eungella via Murwillumbah, NSW 2484, (mail: PO Box 687, Murwillumbah, NSW 2484)/ (066) 72-1903
North Sydney — 180 Falcon St., North Sydney, NSW 2060, (mail: PO Box 459, Cammeray, NSW 2062)/ (02) 959-4558
Perth — 144 Railway Pde., Bayswater. WA 6053. (mail: PO Box 102, Bayswater, WA 6053. (o9) 370-1552

NEW ZEALAND AND FIJI

Auckland, New Zealand—New Varshana, Highway 18, Riverhead, (next to Huapai Golf course) (mail: RD 2 Kumeu, Auckland)/ (9) 412-8075
Christchurch, New Zealand — 83 Bealey Ave., Christchurch, (mail: PO Box 25-190, Christchurch)/ (3) 61-965
Lautoka, Fiji—5 Tavewa Ave., Lautoka (mail: PO Box 125, Lautoka)/ 61-633 ext.48
Suva, Fiji—7 1/2 miles Nasinu (mail: PO Box 6376, Nasinu)/ 39-1282
Wellington, New Zealand—54 David Crescent. Karori/ 04) 764 445

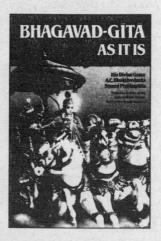

The Hare Krishna Book of
VEGETARIAN COOKING

A colorfully illustrated, practical cookbook that not only helps you prepare authentic Indian dishes at home, but also teaches you about the ancient tradition behind India's world-famous vegetarian cuisine.

130 kitchen-tested recipes, 300 pages, hardback.

US$ 11.60/UK£ 8.95/A$ 15.-

THE HIGHER TASTE
A Guide to Gourmet Vegetarian Cooking and a Karma Free Diet

Illustrated profusely with black and white ink drawings and eight full-colour plates, this popular volume contains over 60 international recipes together with common sense knowledge on the vegetarian life style.

176 pages

US$ 1.65/UK£ 1.00/A$ 2.-

RAJA-VIDYA

THE KING OF KNOWLEDGE

Knowledge of Krishna is absolute and frees the soul from material bondage. It is the perfection of education.

softbound, 128 pages

EASY JOURNEY TO OTHER PLANETS

The *bhakti-yoga* method for transferring oneself from the material to the spiritual world.

softbound, 96 pages

ELEVATION TO KRISHNA CONSCIOUSNESS

God consciousness is the original energy of the living entity, but we are presently in the material concept of life. This book discusses the step by step process of reviving our original peaceful condition.

softbound, 112 pages

KRISHNA CONSCIOUSNESS

THE TOPMOST YOGA SYSTEM

There are many different types of *yoga*. The ultimate object of *yoga* is to understand God/Krishna and this idea is expounded upon for the benefit of the sincere *yoga* student.

softbound, 112 pages

ON THE WAY TO KRISHNA

Describes *bhakti-yoga* methods by practicing which one can attain real happiness.

softbound, 80 pages

Special Offer! All softbound titles on this page, only 1 US$/ 1£/ 2 A$ each.

Keep in Touch . . .

Please send me a free information package and a catalogue of books available.

Name ______________________________

Address ____________________________

____

State ________________ Post Code _____

Return this coupon to:

The Bhaktivedanta Book Trust,
P.O. Box 262 Botany, NSW 2019, Australia

ISKCON Reader Services
P.O. Box 730
Watford, WD25 8ZE
United Kingdom

The Bhaktivedanta Book Trust
3764 Watseka Ave
Los Angeles Oa 90034
U.S.A.

The Bhaktivedanta Book Trust
P.O. Box 56003, Chatsworth Circle, Chatsworth 4020
Durban, South Africa